I

SELENIUM BY EXAMPLE –
VOLUME I: SELENIUM IDE

ISBN: 978-1-291-62456-4

First Edition. First published in 2013.

SELENIUM BY EXAMPLE
Volume I: Selenium IDE

Table of Contents

Contents at a Glance

Table of Contents

Detailed Contents

Chapter 1: Overview of this book.

This chapter lays-out the structure of the rest of the book, as well as giving you details of the notation that is used within the book.

T his chapter sets-out to give you an overview of the rest of this

book, **Selenium By Example – Volume 1: Selenium IDE**, for the purpose of aiding you, the reader, to navigate easier through the rest of the book, to also show the step-by-step approach to learning Selenium IDE that has been taken in the book, and finally to highlight certain notation that is used throughout the book.

1.1 Structure of the book

The structure of the rest of this book is as follows:

- Chapter 2, sets-out to answer the question "what is Selenium IDE". It does this by giving some background on the Selenium project, and a high-level overall of what Selenium IDE is both capable of, and some of the limitations of Selenium IDE.
- Chapter 3, then goes through the process of downloading, installing and then running Selenium IDE for the first-time.
- Chapter 4, introduces Selenium IDE, giving a breakdown of Selenium IDE's user interface and features.
- Chapter 5, identifies the elements (specifically Test Suites, Test Cases, and Test Steps) used within Selenium IDE, giving an explanation of each.
- Chapter 6, then takes you step-by-step through your first recording using Selenium IDE.
- Chapter 7, builds upon the work of Chapter 4, by taking you step-by-step on how to replay and run the recording you completed in Chapter 6.
- Chapter 8, gives a more advanced example of recording and editing a recording.

- Chapter 9, shows you how to export recordings, for use in Selenium Remote Control or Selenium Web Driver.
- Chapter 10, proves an overview of approaches to implementing automated testing using Selenium IDE.

1.2 Notation used in the book

Through-out the rest of this book certain notation is used to aid with the learning of Selenium IDE. This notation is used for highlighting important information you need to know about the item; to warn you of potential problems (you should be aware of); and for providing extra information on the given item (which can be used to find further information).

The following Icons are used for each of these (Important Information, Warnings, and More Information):

 This is the icon used to highlight Important Information you need to know.

 This icon is used to give you Warning information.

 This icon is used to highlight More Information on the topic in hand, or to point you in the right direction to find-out more information on the topic.

1.3 Approach to learning

The aim of this book is to be a step-by-step guide for you to learn, understand, and use Selenium IDE. The approach taken is two prong. Firstly, to break-down the main features into different chapters, building upon the information from previous chapters.

You can see this by the chapter list, where in Chapter 4 we introduce the Selenium IDE user interface, then in Chapter 6 we do our first recording, then in Chapter 7 we re-run our first recording. This approach allows for steady learning in chunks, so you do not get over-loaded with information and forget important information in the process, before you have had a chance to use it practically.

To this, the second prong, is to take a very detailed step-by-step approach through the given task of each chapter. This approach means we have a lot of screenshots (going step-by-step through a given task), you may feel you are able to "jump" pass some of the steps. If you are confident on doing that, that is great, but if you do get lost you can always go back.

1.4 Aim of this book

The aim of this book is that once you have completed reading the book you have a taster of the features of Selenium IDE. This book, like any other book, cannot give you the knowledge/skills you would gain by using Selenium IDE for 1 year/5 years/etc., but it aims to give you a taster of the features of Selenium IDE, and show you how to use them, so you can then get started and use them for yourself.

To make the most of this book you need to down-load and actually use Selenium IDE, to follow through the examples, whilst you go through the book.

Chapter

2

Chapter 2: What is Selenium IDE?

Before we start to use Selenium IDE we need to discuss what Selenium IDE is and more importantly what it can do for you!

hat is Selenium IDE? This is the most important question within this book, and the answer to this question will drive a series of other questions. Before we can start to learn and use Selenium IDE, we first need to discuss several topics around Selenium IDE, these include:

- What Selenium IDE is.
- What Selenium IDE is capable of doing.
- What Selenium IDE is not capable of doing.
- Whether Selenium IDE will be of use to help you.

2.1 What is Selenium IDE

Selenium IDE (or to give it it's proper name Selenium Integrated Development Environment) is a freeware browser plug-in that offers record-and-playback ability allowing you to record actions/inputs/etc., performed against the web-browser; to edit and enhance those recordings; and also to playback the recording to allow the actions/inputs/etc. to be re-performed.

2.1.1 A brief history of Selenium

Selenium was a project originally developed by Jason Huggins of ThoughtWorks in 2004. The decision was made to make Selenium available as open-source software via the Apache 2.0 licence. This product became known as Selenium Server 1.0 (also known as Selenium Remote Control or Selenium RC).

Selenium IDE itself, was developed separately by Shinya Kasatani, who donated Selenium IDE to the main Selenium project in 2006. Selenium IDE was intended to allow users to create automated test scripts for web-browser testing in an easier / non-technical manner compared to Selenium Remote Control.

Selenium IDE, is very simple to use but at the same time has many capabilities. Selenium IDE can be both "as simple as you want it to be" and also "as capable as you need it to be".

2.1.2 Selenium Website

The main website for Selenium is available at the following URL:

http://seleniumhq.org/

The Selenium IDE aspect of the Website is available using the URL:

http://seleniumhq.org/projects/ide/

The documentation for Selenium IDE is available at the following URL:

http://seleniumhq.org/docs/02_selenium_ide.jsp

 You can find-out more information about Selenium IDE at:
http://seleniumhq.org/docs/02_selenium_ide.jsp

2.2 What is Selenium IDE capable of

The next question to ask is: What is Selenium IDE capable of doing? This question is extremely important, as the answer to this question, will drive whether or not Selenium IDE will be of use to you.

Selenium IDE is a very useful tool that is capable of recording the interaction (whether that is via the Keyboard, Mouse, etc.) that a user performs against a Web Page (via a Web Browser).

 Beware that Selenium IDE is only capable of recording and playback using Mozilla Firefox.

These recordings can then be enhanced, altered, played-back to re-perform the actions, split-up into several recordings, added to other recordings, or exported to Selenium Remote Control.

 You can get around the limitation of Selenium IDE only being usable in Mozilla Firefox, by exporting your Recordings to Selenium RC or Selenium Web Driver, which both allow you to run the recordings against any Web Browser.

2.3 What is Selenium IDE not capable of

One question that is worth asking is: What is Selenium IDE not capable of doing? This is important to know, as it will again aid the decision on whether Selenium IDE will be of use to you and help you achieve your objectives for Automated Testing.

The biggest constraint that Selenium IDE has is that the recording and play-back is only possibly in Mozilla Firefox. Depending on the Web Browsers that you need to use to access your Web Page this could be a deciding factor. To this Selenium IDE does not offer either looping or conditional statements.

2.4 Will Selenium IDE be of use to you

This is the most important question and the hardest question to answer, as to truly be able to answer the questions you need to have invested the time and effort to see how useful Selenium IDE will be.

Scenarios where Selenium IDE will be of use to you, are when the challenges you face in your testing, include:-

- The need to repeat manual testing tasks, i.e. performing the same action again and again. *In this case Selenium IDE could be used to record the action and then played-back again and again, to re-perform that action.*

- The User Interface of the website is fairly stable with minimum change likely. *Potentially, ever time the User Interface changes, the Selenium IDE scripts will need to be edited or re-recorded.*

- You have clear scenarios of the functionality to test, and these have clear "routes" through the Web Page. *Whether testing manually or via automation (regardless of whether that is with Selenium IDE or another tool), you need to have clear and concise scenarios to test which have clear "routes" through the web page(s) To put this simply if you cannot state what the expected result is and how to get to the expected result, you cannot hope to be able to automate it.*

2.5 Selenium IDE Version

This book has been written around version 2.4.0 of Selenium IDE. Version 2.4.0 was released on the 16th September 2013.

Chapter 3: Installing Selenium IDE

Before we can start to use Selenium IDE we need to firstly download and install Selenium IDE.

T he most important thing we can do when trying to make a decision on how useful a tool will be to help us to test Web Page(s), is to start using the tool and trying it out. To enable us to do this, obviously we firstly need to download and install the tool. This chapter will take you through the process of downloading and installing Selenium IDE. This chapter concentrates on:

- System requirements for Selenium IDE.
- Downloading Selenium IDE.
- Installing Selenium IDE.
- Running Selenium IDE for the first time.

3.1 System Requirements

To be able to run Selenium IDE, you will need a computer that is capable of running Mozilla Firefox. You can freely download Mozilla Firefox from the below website:

http://www.mozilla.org/en-US/firefox/new

Even if you currently have a version of Morzilla Firefox installed on your machine, it is always advisable to download the most recent version of Mozilla Firefox.

3.2 Downloading Selenium IDE

Let us start by first loading Mozilla Firefox so we are able to download Selenium IDE.

 Beware that Selenium IDE is only capable of recording and playback using Mozilla Firefox.

Firstly, goto the Selenium Website (see Section 2.1 for the URL), from the main page click the **Download** tab (see Figure 3.1).

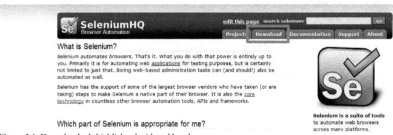

Figure 3.1. Download tab highlighted with red border.

This will load the Selenium Downloads page, from here click the **latest released version number** hyperlink for Selenium IDE (see Figure 3.2).

Figure 3.2. Latest released version number hyperlink for Selenium IDE, highlighted with red border.

Clicking the **latest release version number** hyperlink will load a pop-up dialog (see Figure 3.3) asking you to allow the installation of the software on your computer, please click the **Allow** Button (see Figure 3.4).

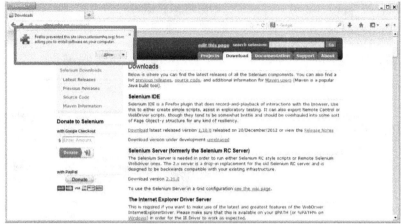

Figure 3.3. This Pop-up dialog may be shown when you download Selenium IDE.

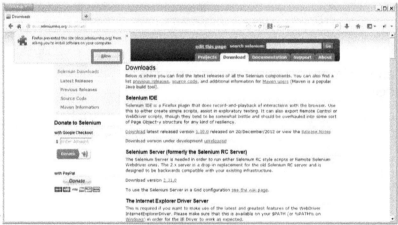

Figure 3.4. If the pop-up dialog does appear click the **Allow** Button, highlighted with red border.

3.3 Installing Selenium IDE

Once you have allowed the download to begin, a **Software Installation** Dialog will appear (see Figure 3.5). This will offer you 5 items to install, please click the **Install Now** Button (see Figure 3.6).

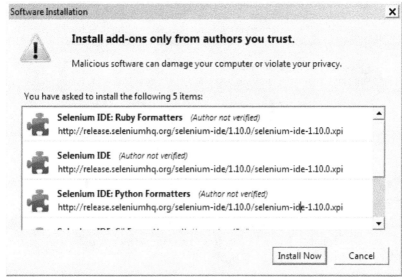

Figure 3.5. The Software Installation Dialog.

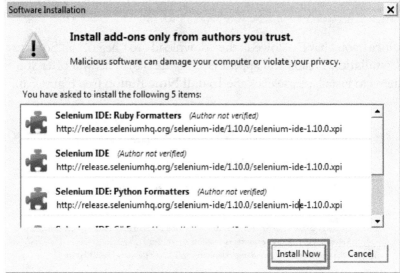

Figure 3.6. The **Install Now** Button highlighted with a red border.

After downloading and installing the Selenium IDE components, Mozilla Firefox will ask you to allow it to restart (see Figure 3.7). When the Restart Mozilla Firefox message appears please click the **Restart Now** Button (see Figure 3.8).

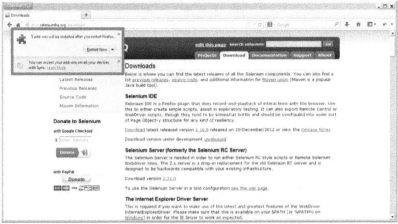

Figure 3.7. The Mozilla Firefox Pop-Up asking to restart Mozilla Firefox (highlighted in red).

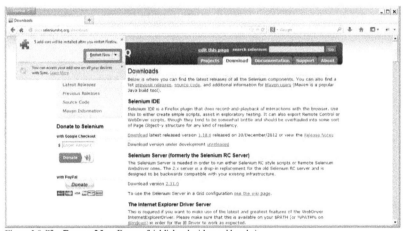

Figure 3.8. The **Restart Now** Button (highlighted with a red border).

Clicking the **Restart Now** Button will close Mozilla Firefox and the re-open it. Now let us confirm that Selenium IDE has been installed into Mozilla Firefox, click the **Firefox** Menu (see Figure 3.9).

Figure 3.9. The **Firefox** Menu highlighted with red border.

Once you have clicked the **Firefox** Menu move your cursor down to the **Web Developer** Menu Item (see Figure 3.10). This will load the Web Developer Sub-Menu, and there should be a **Selenium IDE** Menu Item (see Figure 3.11).

Figure 3.10. The **Web Developer** Menu Item highlighted with a red border.

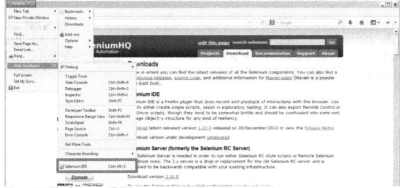

Figure 3.11. The **Selenium IDE** Menu Item highlighted with a red border.

3.4 Running Selenium for the first time

Let us now run Selenium IDE for the first time, to ensure it loads correctly. Click the **Firefox** Menu and select the **Web Developer** Menu Item and finally click the **Selenium IDE** Menu Item (**Firefox Menu** > **Web Developer** Menu > **Selenium IDE** Menu Item). This should load the **Selenium IDE** (as shown in Figure 3.12) in a separate window.

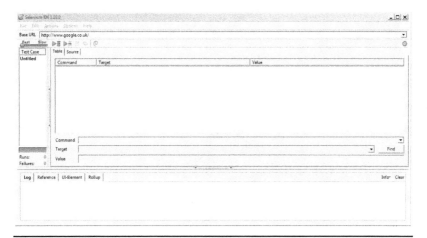

Figure 3.12. The **Selenium IDE** window.

Alternatively, within Mozilla Firefox you are able to load the Selenium IDE dialog by holding down the **Ctrl** and **Alt** keys and then pressing the **S** key.

Hold down the  keys, and then press the key.

 To quickly load the Selenium IDE dialog from within Mozilla Firefox, hold down the **Ctrl** and **Alt** keys and then press the **S** key.

In the next chapter, Chapter 4 (The Selenium IDE), we will go through the Selenium Integrated Development Environment, providing an overview of each feature available.

Chapter

4

Chapter 4: The Selenium IDE

This chapter provides an overview of the Selenium IDE user interface, taking in each feature.

L et us go into detail around the Selenium Integrated

Development Environment (IDE), and the features available within Selenium IDE. This chapter will take you through each option of Selenium IDE, including:

- Selenium IDE overview.
- File Menu options.
- Edit Menu options.
- Actions Menu options.
- Options Menu options.
- Help Menu options.

4.1 Selenium IDE dialog

Let us run the Selenium IDE dialog (either via the **Firefox** Menu > **Web Developer** Menu Item > **Selenium IDE** Menu Item or via holding **Ctrl** + **Alt** and pressing the **S** key). This will load the **Selenium IDE** as shown in Figure 4.1 below.

Figure 4.1. The **Selenium IDE**.

The Selenium IDE is made up of several areas, firstly is the Menu Bar (Figure 4.2). Next is the Toolbar (Figure 4.3). Then it is Test Case List (Figure 4.4), after this is the Test Step Pane (Figure 4.5), then next is the Output Pane (Figure 4.6).

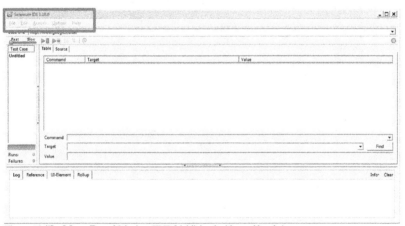

Figure 4.2. The **Menu Bar** of Selenium IDE (highlighted with a red border).

Figure 4.3. The **Tool Bar** of Selenium IDE (highlighted with a red border).

Figure 4.4. The **Test Case List** of Selenium IDE (highlighted with a red border).

Figure 4.5. The **Test Step** Pane of Selenium IDE (highlighted with a red border).

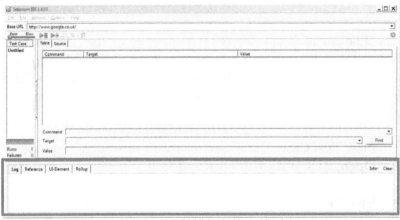

Figure 4.6. The **Output** Pane of Selenium IDE (highlighted with a red border).

4.2 Selenium IDE elements

In this section we will go through each of the elements of the Selenium IDE in more detail. The elements are shown in Figures 4.2 through 4.6.

4.3   Selenium IDE Menu elements

Selenium IDE has the following Menu items:-

- **File.**
- **Edit.**
- **Actions.**
- **Options.**
- **Help.**

Each of these Menu items have a series of Menu options / Sub-Menu items.

4.3.1   The File Menu

The **File** Menu (quick access by holding down the "**Alt**" Key + pressing the "**F**" Key), has two main sections: those relating to Test Cases and those related to Test Suites. Chapter 5, goes into detail around Test Suites, Test Cases, and Test Steps. The File Menu has the following Menu items:

- **New Test Case**: This is used to create a new blank Test Case.
- **Open**: This is used to open and load a previously saved Test Case.
- **Save Test Case**: This allows you to save the current Test Case.
- **Save Test Case As**: This allows you to save the current Test Case, specifying a name for the file.
- **Export Test Case As**: This allows you to export the Test Case into a series of Languages (Ruby/Python/Java/C#) in both Selenium Remote Control and Selenium WebDriver formats.
- **Recent Test Cases**: This lists the last saved Test Cases (clicking on each will allow you to quickly load the selected Test Case).
- **Add Test Case**: This allows you to search for and load a Test Case into the currently opened Test Case, so as to merge them.

- **Properties**: This will give you properties of the current Test Case you are working on (including the Name of the Test Case and Filename of the stored file). More information on the Properties is given in Section 4.5.2.
- **New Test Suite**: This is used to create a new blank Test Suite.
- **Open**: This is used to open and load a previously saved Test Suite.
- **Save Test Suite**: This allows you to save a Test Suite.
- **Save Test Suite As**: This allows you to save a Test Suite, specifying a name for the file.
- **Export Test Suite As**: This allows you to export the Test Suite into a series of Languages (Ruby/Python/Java/C#) in both Selenium Remote Control and Selenium WebDriver format.
- **Recent Test Suites**: This lists the last saved Test Suites, clicking on each item will allow you to quickly load that Test Suite.
- **Close (X)**: This closes the Selenium IDE Dialog.

4.3.2 The Edit Menu

The **Edit** Menu (quick access by holding down the "**Alt**" Key + pressing the "**E**" Key) has the following Menu items:

- **Undo**: This undoes the last action you performed. It can be used to undo a series of actions.
- **Redo**: This re-does the last undo action (if you have previously undo the last action). Again, this can be used to redo a series of undone actions.
- **Cut**: This cuts the currently selected item copying it into the Clipboard (allowing you to paste it to another location), and removing it from the current location.
- **Copy**: This makes a copy the currently selected item copying it into the Clipboard (allowing you to paste it). The item remains in the current location.

- **Paste**: This allows you to Paste the item in the Clipboard to the current location (assuming you have used either the Cut or Copy options to place an element into the Clipboard).
- **Delete**: This deletes the currently selected item, removing it from the current location.
- **Select All**: This will select (highlight) all the items. This is helpful if you want to Cut, Copy, or Delete all items.
- **Insert New Command**: This will insert a blank row in the Test Step Pane (see Figure 4.5) at the currently selected location, to allow you to create a new Command.
- **Insert New Comment**: This will insert a blank row in the Test Step Pane (see Figure 4.5) at the currently selected location, to allow you to create a new Comment.

4.3.4 The Actions Menu

The **Actions** Menu (quick access by holding down the "**Alt**" Key + pressing the "**A**" Key) has the following Menu items:

- **Record**: This will start to "record" the actions you perform (e.g. interactions via the Mouse and Keyboard) with the Web Page via the Firefox Web Browser. When recording this Menu Item displays a tick against it.
- **Play entire test suite**: This option will play-back (re-run) every Test Case in the Test Case List (Figure 4.4), starting at the top and running through to the bottom of the list.
- **Play current test case**: This option will play-back (re-run) the currently selected Test Case in the Test Case List (Figure 4.4).
- **Pause / Resume**: This option will Pause (temporary stop the play-back of the Test Cases) or Resume (continue the play-back of the Test Cases).
- **Step**: This option allows you to "step through" the playing-back of the Test Case (this works with the Breakpoints, etc.) This is useful for debugging purposes.

- **Fastest (0)**: This sets the play-back speed to be the fastest play-back speed (Speed = 0), so the play-back (re-running) of the Test Cases takes the shortest amount of time.
- **Faster (-)**: This speeds-up the play-back (re-running) of the Test Case, so it takes less time to run the Test Cases.
- **Slower (+)**: This slows-down the play-back (re-running) of the Test Case, so it takes more time to run the Test Cases.
- **Slowest (9)**: This sets the play-back speed to be the slowest play-back speed (Speed = 9), so the play-back (re-running) of the Test Cases takes the longest amount of time.
- **Toggle Breakpoint**: This sets the currently selected row of the Test Step as a Breakpoint, meaning that the play-back (re-running) pauses on that Command. To show that the Command has a Breakpoint (a Yellow Pause Icon is displayed against that Command).
- **Set / Clear Start Point**: This sets/clears the currently selected row of the Test Step as the Start Point, meaning that the play-back (re-running) starts from that Command. To show that the Command has a Start Point (a Green Start Icon is displayed against that Command).
- **Execute this command**: This option will play-back (re-run) just the selected Command in isolation.

4.3.5 The Options Menu

The **Options** Menu (quick access by holding down the "**Alt**" Key + pressing the "**O**" Key) has the following Menu items:

- **Options**: This loads the Option Dialog, allowing you to setup various aspects of the Recordings and Save File settings. See Section 4.3.7 for more information on the Options Dialog.
- **Format**: This allows you to use the old formatting provided by Selenium IDE.

- **Clipboard Format**: This allows you to select the Language (HTML/Ruby/Python/Java/C#) and Format (Selenium Remote Control/Selenium WebDriver) that will be used by the Clipboard (when you Cut, Copy, Paste Commands).
- **Reset IDE Window**: This resets the IDE Window to the default size and default elements, over-writing the sizes and configuration you have specified and setup during your usage of Selenium IDE.
- **Clear History**: This clears the history (Base URL, Test Cases, and Test Suites). This option is only available when you have a Base URL and at least one Test Case.

4.3.6 The Help Menu

The Help Menu has the following Menu items:

- **Documentation**: This takes you to the **Documentation** area of the official Selenium website:
  http://docs.seleniumhq.org/docs/02_selenium_ide.jsp
- **UI-Element Documentation**: This loads the **UI-Element Documentation** section of your local Selenium IDE area:
  chrome://selenium-ide/content/selenium-core/scripts/ui.doc.html
- **Report Issue**: This takes you to a website allowing you to report issues (defects) you have encountered during your usage of Selenium IDE.
- **Release Notes**: This takes you to the **Release Note** area of the official Selenium website:
  http://code.google.com/p/selenium/wiki/SeIDEReleaseNotes
- **Official Selenium Blog**: This takes you to the Selenium Blog website.
  http://seleniumhq.wordpress.com/
- **Official Selenium Website**: This takes you to the Selenium website:
  http://docs.seleniumhq.org/

4.3.7   The Options Dialog

The **Options** Menu Item (**Options** Menu > **Options...** Menu Item) loads the Selenium IDE Options Dialog (as shown in Figure 4.7).

The Options Dialog has the following Tabs:

- **General.**
- **Formats.**
- **Plugins.**
- **Locator Builders.**
- **WebDriver.**

The Options Dialog also has the following Buttons:

- **Reset Options.**
- **OK.**
- **Cancel.**

The **Reset Options** Button is used to reset the options used in Selenium IDE to the default settings that are recommend for Selenium IDE. This will over-write any settings you have setup in Selenium IDE. The **OK** Button is used to Save any changes you have made on the Options Dialog and then close the Options Dialog. The **Cancel** Button is used to close the Options Dialog without saving any changes you have made.

4.3.8   The Options Dialog > General Tab

The Options Dialog > **General** Tab as shown in Figure 4.8, allows you to setup various general settings for Selenium IDE, such as Text File Encodings, Timeouts, any Selenium IDE Extensions, whether to remember URLs, etc.

4.3.9 The Options Dialog > Formats Tab

The Options Dialog > **Formats** Tab as shown in Figure 4.9, allows you to set the Formats that you can export Test Cases to. Initially, Selenium IDE comes with various Formats including: HTML, Ruby, Python, Java, and C# (in both Selenium Remote Control and Selenium WebDriver formats). The Formats Tab also allows you to Add a new Format, update an existing Format, Rename an existing Format, Delete an existing Format, and view the Source code for a Format.

4.3.10 The Options Dialog > Plugins Tab

The Options Dialog > **Plugins** Tab as shown in Figure 4.10, allows you to view and disable any of the plugins that have been added to Selenium IDE. Selenium IDE initially comes with plugins for the following Formats: Ruby, Python, Java, and C#.

4.3.11 The Options Dialog > Locator Builders Tab

The Options Dialog > **Locator Builders** Tab as shown in Figure 4.11, allows you to view and re-order the elements of the builders that show the locator information (e.g. ui, id, link, etc.) You can use this to change which order the elements are used to locate Web Page elements in.

4.3.11 The Options Dialog > WebDriver Tab

The Options Dialog > **WebDriver** Tab as shown in Figure 4.12, allows you to turn on/off Selenium WebDriver play-back and also to specify the Web Browser (all popular Web Browsers are supported), that Selenium WebDriver will use to play-back the Test Suites/Test Cases.

This option (although currently as of December 2013, is still experimental) will allow play-back of your recordings in Selenium WebDriver directly via Selenium IDE.

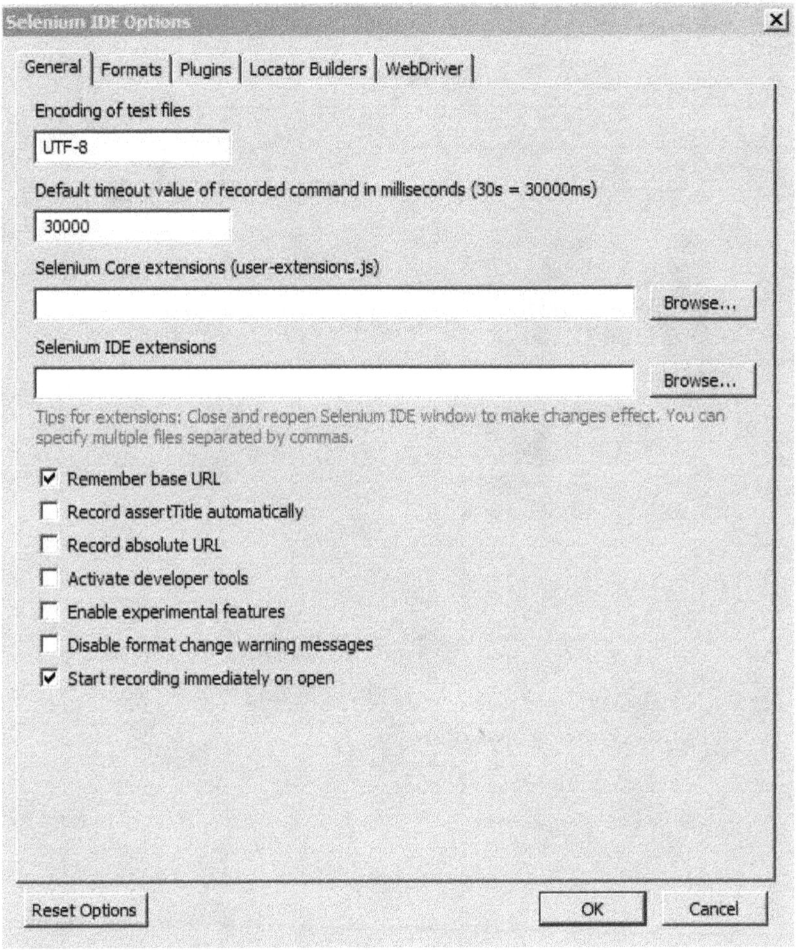

Figure 4.7. The **Options** Dialog.

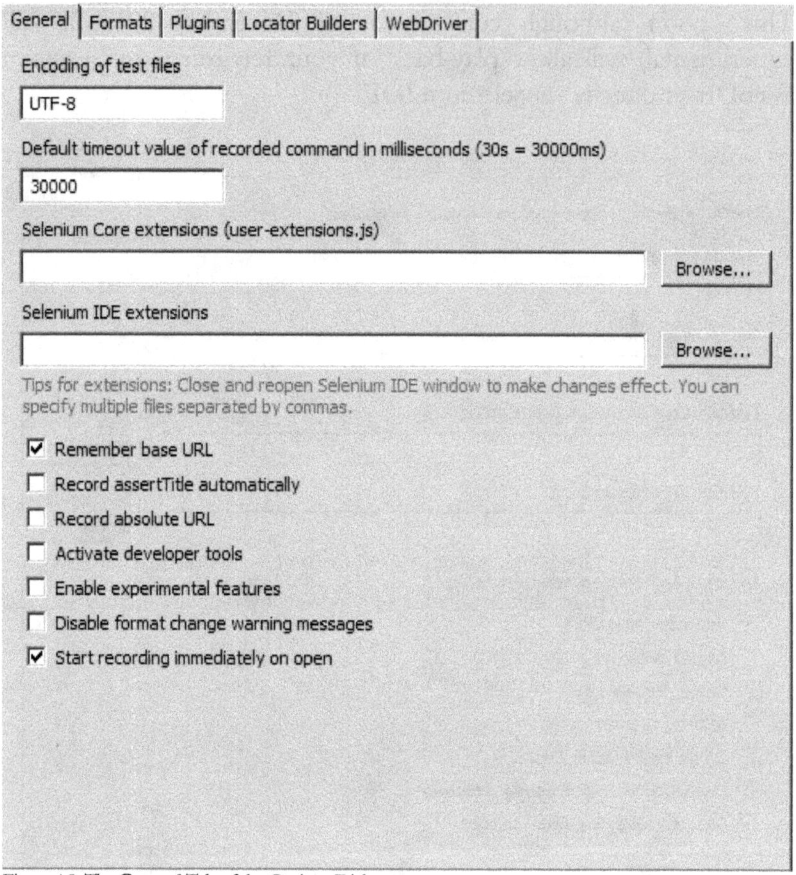

General | Formats | Plugins | Locator Builders | WebDriver |

Encoding of test files

UTF-8

Default timeout value of recorded command in milliseconds (30s = 30000ms)

30000

Selenium Core extensions (user-extensions.js)

[ ] Browse...

Selenium IDE extensions

[ ] Browse...

Tips for extensions: Close and reopen Selenium IDE window to make changes effect. You can specify multiple files separated by commas.

☑ Remember base URL

☐ Record assertTitle automatically

☐ Record absolute URL

☐ Activate developer tools

☐ Enable experimental features

☐ Disable format change warning messages

☑ Start recording immediately on open

Figure 4.8. The **General** Tab of the Options Dialog.

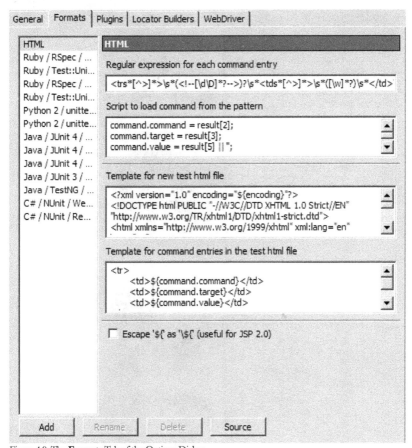

Figure 4.9. The **Formats** Tab of the Options Dialog.

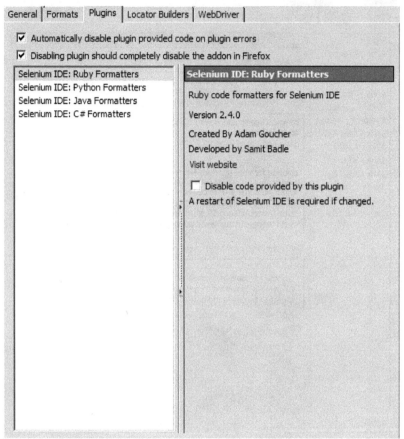

Figure 4.10. The **Plugins** Tab of the Options Dialog.

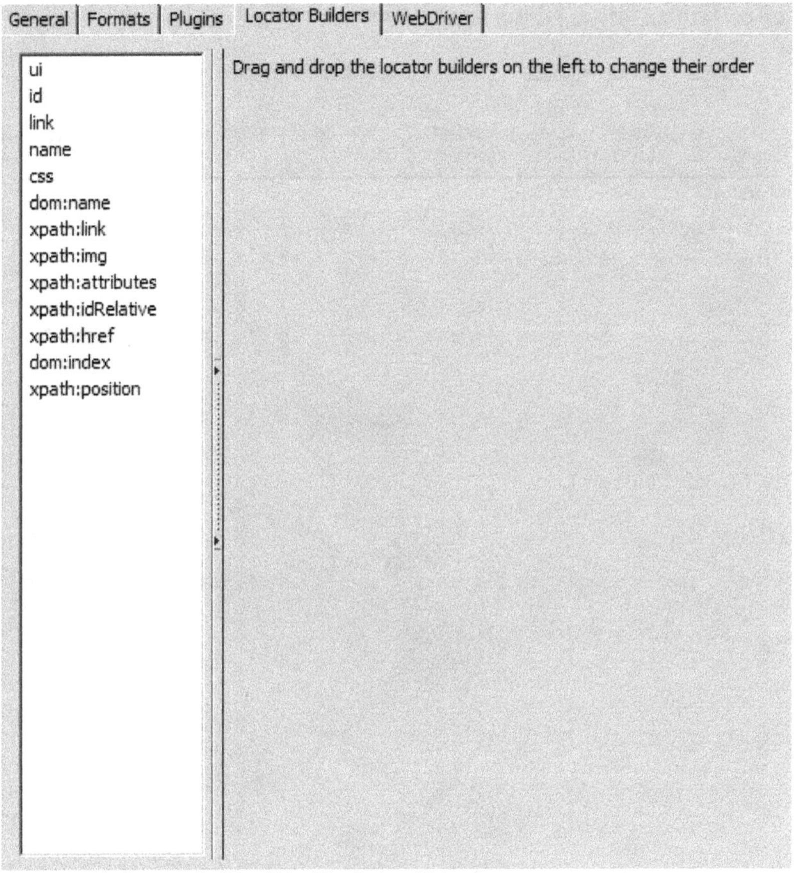

| General | Formats | Plugins | Locator Builders | WebDriver |

```
ui
id
link
name
css
dom:name
xpath:link
xpath:img
xpath:attributes
xpath:idRelative
xpath:href
dom:index
xpath:position
```

Drag and drop the locator builders on the left to change their order

Figure 4.11. The **Locator Builders** Tab of the Options Dialog.

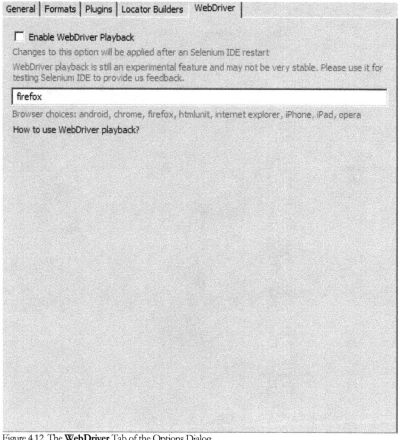

General | Formats | Plugins | Locator Builders | WebDriver |

☐ Enable WebDriver Playback

Changes to this option will be applied after an Selenium IDE restart

WebDriver playback is still an experimental feature and may not be very stable. Please use it for testing Selenium IDE to provide us feedback.

firefox

Browser choices: android, chrome, firefox, htmlunit, internet explorer, iPhone, iPad, opera

How to use WebDriver playback?

Figure 4.12. The **WebDriver** Tab of the Options Dialog.

4.4 Selenium IDE Toolbar elements

The Selenium IDE Toolbar (Figure 4.3) has the following Buttons to allow you to quickly access Menu Options:

- **Base URL** Combobox.
- **Speed** Slider.
- **Play Entire Test Suite** Button.

- **Pause / Resume** Button.
- **Step** Button.
- **Apply Rollup Rules** Button.

4.4.1 Base URL Combobox

The **Base URL** Combobox as shown in Figure 4.13, shows the Base URL (URL which is the starting point for your recordings).

Figure 4.13. The **Base URL** Combobox.

Each time you start a new recording against a different URL, that URL will be added to the Base URL Combobox, so you can re-use the URL in future for that recording. The Base URL also allows you to type a URL directly into the Textbox element of the Base URL Combobox.

4.4.2 Speed Slider

The **Speed** Slider as shown in Figure 4.14, allows you to set the speed of play-back from the fastest setting (speed = 0) to the slowest setting (speed = 9). The Speed Slider effectively allows you to do the same tasks as using the **Actions** Menu > **Fastest (0)** Menu Item, **Actions** Menu > **Faster** Menu Item, **Actions** Menu > **Slower** Menu Item, **Actions** Menu > **Slowest (9)** Menu Item.

The Speed Slider allows you to change the play-back speed quicker, and with more flexibility that using the Menu Items.

Figure 4.14. The **Speed** Slider.

You use the Speed Slider by moving the Green Round Button to the left (to make play-back faster) or to the right (to make play-back slower).

4.4.3   Play Entire Test Suite Button

The **Play Entire Test Suite** Button as shown in Figure 4.15, allows you to run (play-back) all the Test Cases shown in the Test Case List (Figure 4.4). The Play Entire Test Suite Button is the same as selecting the **Actions** Menu > **Play entire test suite** Menu Item.

Figure 4.15. The **Play Entire Test Suite** Button.

You can use the Play Entire Test Suite Button to quickly run (play-back) all the Test Cases within the Test Case List.

4.4.4   Play Current Test Case Button

The **Play Current Test Case** Button as shown in Figure 4.16, is used to run (play-back) the currently selected Test Case in the Test Case List (Figure 4.4). The Play Current Test Case Button is a quick way of using the **Actions** Menu > **Play current test case** Menu Item.

Figure 4.16. The **Play Current Test Case** Button.

You can use the Play Current Test Case Button to execute just the selected Test Case in the Test Case List.

4.4.5 Pause / Resume Button

The **Pause / Resume** Button as shown in Figures 4.17 and 4.18, allows you to either Pause (when play-back of Test Cases is running) or Resume (when play-back of Test Cases is paused). The Pause / Resume Button is a quick way of using the **Actions** Menu > **Pause / Resume** Menu Item.

Figure 4.17. The **Pause / Resume** Button (this icon is displayed when play-back is running).

Figure 4.18. The **Pause / Resume** Button (this icon is displayed when when play-back is paused).

The Pause / Resume Button effectively works as a toggle. When play-back of Test Cases is currently running, the Pause / Resume Button has the icon shown in Figure 4.17, and when clicked is used to Pause (temporarily stop) the play-back. However, when play-back of Test Cases is currently paused, the Pause / Resume Button has the icon shown in Figure 4.18, and when clicked is used to Resume (continue) the play-back.

4.4.6 Step Button

The **Step** Button as shown in Figure 4.19, is used to step through the Test Step Commands in the Test Step Pane (Figure 4.5). The Step Button is a quick way of using the **Actions** Menu > **Step** Menu Item.

Figure 4.19. The **Step** Button.

The Step Button is only usable (enabled so the button can be clicked on) when the play-back of the Test Cases is paused (by using the Pause / Resume Button). The Step Button allows you to step through each of the Commands in the Test Step Pane one command at a time. This is very useful for debugging a Test Case.

4.4.7 Apply Rollup Rules Button

The **Apply Rollup Rules** Button as shown in Figure 4.20, allows you to roll-up all the rules that have been used in the Test Suite/Test Cases.

Figure 4.20. The **Apply Rollup Rules** Button.

4.4.8 Record Button

The **Record** Button as shown in Figure 4.21, allows you to start or stop the recording of the interaction (mouse clicks, key presses, etc.) within the Web Browser. The Record Button is a quick way of using the **Actions** Menu > **Record** Menu Item.

Figure 4.21. The **Record** Button.

The Record Button works as a toggle. When there is no recording happening, the Record Button is enabled (and the Actions Menu > Record Menu Item does not display a Tick against it). If you then click the Record Button it will then **start** recording the interaction (mouse clicks, key presses, etc.) within the Web Browser and also adds a Tick to the Actions Menu > Record Menu Item.

When there is a recording happening, the Record Button is enabled (and the Actions Menu > Record Menu Item does have a Tick shown against it). If you then click the Record Button it will then **stop** recording the interaction (mouse clicks, key presses, etc.) within the Web Browser and also remove the Tick that was shown on the Actions Menu > Record Menu Item.

4.5 Test Case List

The **Test Case** List (Figure 4.22) lists all the Test Cases that you have created.

Figure 4.22. The **Test Case** List.

The Test Cases are listed in the order you created/loaded/added them to the Test Suite (Chapter 5 goes into more detail about the differences between Test Suites, Test Cases, and Test Steps).

When you add a new Test Case (**File** Menu > **New Test Case** Menu Item) it is added as "**Untitled**" (then "**Untitled 2**", "**Untitled 3**", etc.) When you name the Test Case by choosing the **File** Menu > **Save Test Case** Menu Item (or by holding down the **CTRL** Key and pressing the **S** Key), the name is updated in the Test Case List.

At any point you can re-order the Test Cases by selecting a Test Case (and whilst holding the Left-Mouse Key down) dragging it to another location, in the Test Case List.

The Test Case that is selected and has its' Commands shown in the Test Step Pane (Figure 4.5) will have its' name shown in bold text. In Figure 4.23, the Test Case named **Google-Search-2** is in bold, as it is the selected Test Case and it's Test Steps are shown in the Test Step Pane.

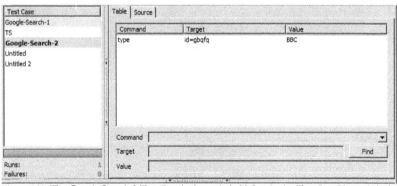

Figure 4.23. The **Google-Search-2** Test Case is shown in bold font in the Test Case List, as it is the selected Test Case.

SELENIUM BY EXAMPLE - VOLUME I: SELENIUM IDE

Below the list of Test Cases, are two import Labels (Runs and Failures). The **Runs** Label shows the number of Test Cases that have been ran (played-back), whilst the **Failures** Label shows you how many of the Test Cases failed when they were ran (played-back). These values are updated with each play-back run

4.5.1 Quick Access Menu

If you Right-Hand Mouse Click anywhere in the Test Case List it will load the Quick Access Menu as shown in Figure 4.24). This will allow the following Menu options:

- **New Test Case.**
- **Add Test Case.**
- **Delete.**
- **Properties.**

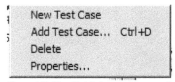

Figure 4.24. The **Quick Access** Menu on the Test Case List.

The **New Test Case** option, is a short-cut for choosing **File** Menu > **New Test Case** Menu Item, and allows you to add a new blank Test Case.

The **Add Test Case** option, is a short-cut for choosing **File** Menu > **Add Test Case** Menu Item, and allows you to add an existing Test Case.

The **Delete** option allows you to delete the selected Test Cases (this is the same as using the **Edit** Menu > **Delete** Menu Item).

The **Properties** option is a short-cut for using **File** Menu > **Properties** Menu Item, and allows you to view the Properties of the selected Test Case in the Test Case List.

4.5.2 Test Case Property Dialog

The **Properties** Dialog as shown in Figure 4.25, has two Fields (**File** and **Title**). The File field shows the Filename of the stored Test Case. The Title field shows the name of the Test Case (as shown in the Test Case List).

You can change the value in the Title field, which allows you to rename the Test Case.

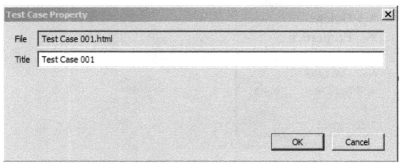

Figure 4.25. The **Test Case Property** Dialog.

4.6 Test Step Pane

The **Test Step** Pane (Figure 4.26) lists all Test Step Commands of the selected Test Cases.

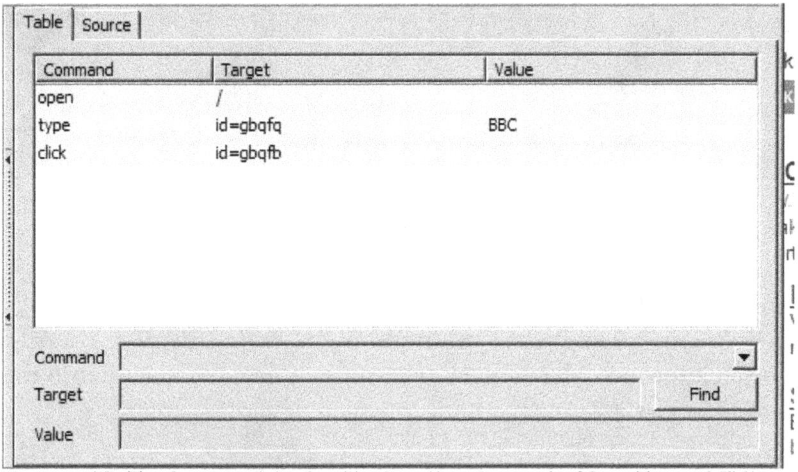

Figure 4.26. The **Test Step** Pane, listing three Test Steps (three Commands of Open, Type, and Click).

The Test Step Pane is made-up of two Tabs, **Table** and **Source**. Both Tabs are used to view the Test Case's Test Step(s) in different formats.

4.6.1 The Table Tab

The **Table** Tab shows the Test Case's Commands (Test Step). The Table Tab has two sections, firstly, a list of the Test Steps (Commands), as shown in Figure 4.27. Secondly is the Command Section (as shown in Figure 4.28).

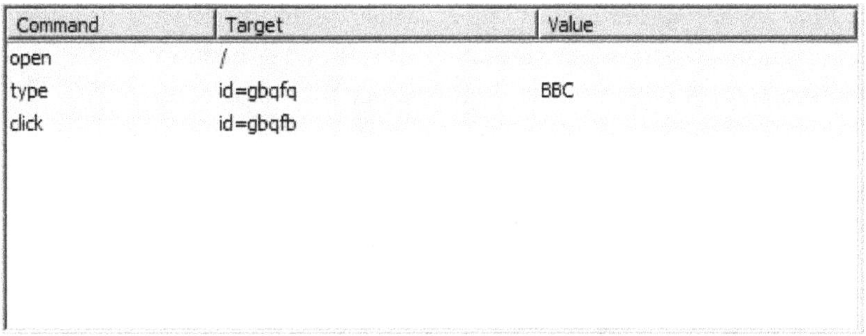

Figure 4.27. The List of Test Steps (Commands). In this case there are three Test Steps **Open, Type, and Click**.

Command	open	▼
Target	/	Find
Value		

Figure 4.28. The **Command Section** of the Table Tab.

The Test Steps List (Figure 4.27) allows you to add (via recording, **Edit** Menu > **Add New Command** Menu Item, **Edit** Menu > **Add New Comment** Menu Item, or Pasting) a new Command into the Test Step List.

The Command Section (Figure 4.28), allows you to alter the Command, Target (UI Elements), or Value of a Test Step.

The **Command** Combobox (as shown in Figure 4.29) lists all the available Selenium IDE Commands, that can be used in a Test Step.

The **Target** Combobox (as shown in Figure 4.30) lists all the Locators (ways Selenium IDE uses to identify User Interface elements), this is commonly HTML Tags for id, name, css, or via Document Object Model or XPath.

The **Find** Button (as shown in Figure 4.31) allows you to identify items on a Web Page.

The **Value** Textbox (as shown in Figure 4.32) allows you to set a value to use, for example the text to enter for a type command.

Figure 4.29. The list of available Selenium IDE Commands in the **Command** Combobox.

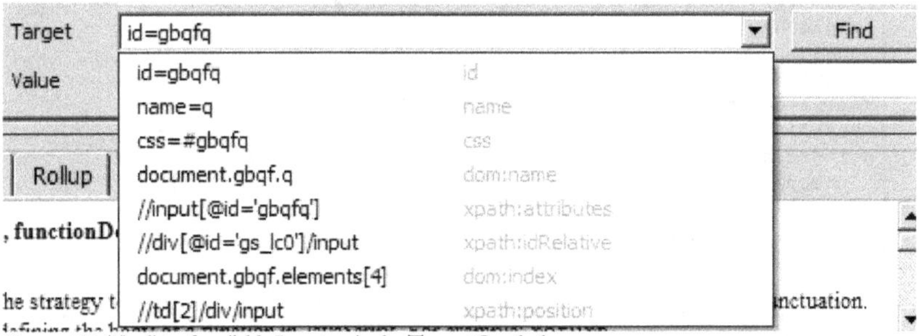

Figure 4.30. The list of available Locators in the **Target** Combobox.

Figure 4.31. The **Find** Button.

Figure 4.32. The **Value** Textbox.

4.6.2 The Source Tab

The **Source** Tab (Figure 4.33) shows you the Test Step(s) in source code format. By default this is HTML, but can be changed by using the Options Dialog. You can edit the text in the Source Tab, and when you then go back to the Table Tab the Test Steps/Commands will be updated to show the alterations.

The Source Tab works as a normal text editor, allowing you to make alterations quickly and simply.

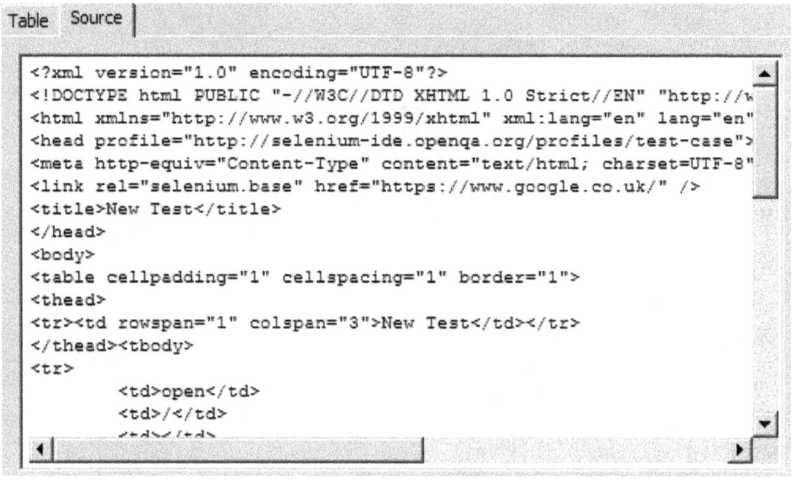

```
Table  Source

<?xml version="1.0" encoding="UTF-8"?>
<!DOCTYPE html PUBLIC "-//W3C//DTD XHTML 1.0 Strict//EN" "http://w
<html xmlns="http://www.w3.org/1999/xhtml" xml:lang="en" lang="en"
<head profile="http://selenium-ide.openqa.org/profiles/test-case">
<meta http-equiv="Content-Type" content="text/html; charset=UTF-8"
<link rel="selenium.base" href="https://www.google.co.uk/" />
<title>New Test</title>
</head>
<body>
<table cellpadding="1" cellspacing="1" border="1">
<thead>
<tr><td rowspan="1" colspan="3">New Test</td></tr>
</thead><tbody>
<tr>
        <td>open</td>
        <td>/</td>
        <td></td>
```

Figure 4.33. The **Source** Tab showing the Test Step(s) in HTML format.

4.6.3 Quick Access Menu (Table Tab)

If you Right-Hand Mouse Click anywhere in the Table Tab, you get a Quick Access Menu (as shown in Figure 4.34). This provides the following Menu Items:

- **Cut.**
- **Copy.**

- Paste.
- Delete.
- Insert New Command.
- Insert New Comment.
- Clear All.
- Toggle Breakpoint.
- Set / Clear Start Point.
- Execute This Command.

Each of the Quick Access Menu options Item corresponds to a Menu Item from either the **Edit** Menu or **Actions** Menu.

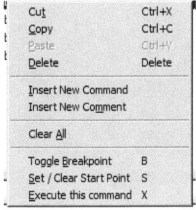

Figure 4.34. The **Quick Access** Menu from the Table Tab.

4.6.4 Quick Access Menu (Source Tab)

If you Right-Hand Mouse Click anywhere in the Source Tab, you get a Quick Access Menu (as shown in Figure 4.35). This provides the following Menu Items:

- Undo.
- Cut.
- Copy.

- Paste.
- Delete.
- Select All.

Each of the Quick Access Menu Item corresponds to a Menu Item from the **Edit** Menu.

Figure 4.35. The **Quick Access** Menu from the Source Tab.

4.7 Output Pane

The **Output Pane** (Figures 4.6 and 4.36) provides important information about the Test Step. The Output Pane has four Tabs:

- Log.
- Reference.
- UI-Element.
- Rollup.

Figure 4.36. The **Output** Pane.

4.7.1 The Log Tab

The **Log** Tab (as shown in Figure 4.37) list an on-going Log associated with this Test Suite/Test Case. It lists four types of Messages:

- **Debug.**
- **Info.**
- **Warn.**
- **Error.**

You can filter to show any or all of them by using the **Info** Button Menu (as shown in Figure 4.38), and selecting one of the information types, for example Figure 4.39 is showing just messages of type Error. You can also use the **Clear** Button (as shown in Figure 4.40) to clear all the Messages.

Figure 4.37. The **Log** Tab of the Output Pane.

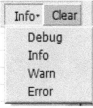

Figure 4.38. The **Info** Button Menu.

Figure 4.39. The **Log** Tab showing only **Error Type** Messages.

Figure 4.40. The **Clear** Button.

4.7.2 The Reference Tab

The **Reference** Tab, as shown on Figure 4.41 gives you information about the Command that is currently selected in the Test Step. This provides quick help, telling you a little about the Command and the arguments the Command requires.

For example the Command being used in Figure 4.42 is the **click** Command (for clicking on Buttons etc.)

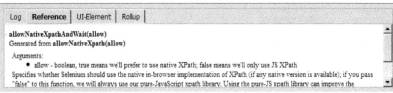

Figure 4.41. The **Reference** Tab.

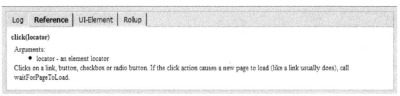

Figure 4.42. The **Reference** Tab showing information for the **click** Command.

4.7.3 The UI-Element Tab

The **UI-Element** Tab, as shown on Figure 4.43 shows information about the UI Element that is used in your Test Step.

| Log | Reference | **UI-Element** | Rollup |

Figure 4.43. The **UI-Element** Tab.

4.7.4 The Rollup Tab

The **Rollup** Tab, as shown on Figure 4.44 shows information on the rollup associated with your Test Step. This relates to the Apply Rollup Rules Button (please see Section 4.4.7).

| Log | Reference | UI-Element | **Rollup** |

Figure 4.44. The **Rollup** Tab.

Chapter 5: Test Suite, Test Case, and Test Step

We now define a Test Suite, Test Case and Test Step, and how these relate to Commands and Comments.

Before we start our first recording lets define some of the important elements and how they relate to each other in Selenium IDE. In this chapter will define the following elements:

- Test Suite.
- Test Case.
- Test Step.

5.1 Test Suite

Test Suites are made-up of one or more Test Cases. All the Test Cases in a Test Suite should in some-way relate to each other (from a Website Functionality testing point-of-view).

From a Selenium IDE point-of-view, the Test Suite can be thought of as the list of Test Cases. In Figure 5.1, all of the Test Cases (Test Case 001, Test Case 002, Test Case 003, Test Case 004, and Test Case 005) make-up a single Test Suite.

Test Suites are optional in Selenium IDE, in that you could have one very large Test Case, or a series of Test Cases without a Test Suite. This approach will work, but will make re-using and managing Test Cases much harder.

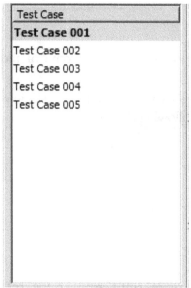

Figure 5.1. The above Test Cases (Test Case 001, Test Case 002, Test Case 003, Test Case 004, and Test Case 005) are all part of one **Test Suite**.

5.2 Test Case

Test Cases are made-up of one or more Test Steps. Each Test Case is separate and can be ran (played-back), edited, saved, etc. in isolation of other Test Cases.

From a Selenium IDE point-of-view (using Figure 5.2), the Test Case **Test Case 003** can be used in complete isolation of the other Test Cases. Although part of the same Test Suite, each of the Test Cases is it's own individual entity.

Test Case
Test Case 001
Test Case 002
Test Case 003
Test Case 004
Test Case 005

Figure 5.2. The above **Test Cases** (Test Case 001, Test Case 002, Test Case 003, Test Case 004, and Test Case 005) are all separate entities, which can work in isolation or together.

5.3 Test Step

Test Steps are the actual commands that will be executed. Each Test Case is made-up of one or more Test Steps.

From a Selenium IDE point-of-view (using Figure 5.3), each row in the Table (e.g. each Command: **Open, Type, Click, AddLocationStrategy**, or **AddLocationStrategy**), is a single Test Step. Test Steps work together, each follows the last.

Command	Target	Value
open	/	
type	id=gbqfq	BBC
click	id=gbqfb	
addLocationStrategy	id=gbqfq	BBC
addLocationStrategy	id=gbqfq	BBC2

Figure 5.3. The above **Test Steps** (e.g. each Command: Open, Type, Click, AddLocationStrategy, and AddLocationStrategy) work together.

5.4 Relationship Hierarchy

The relationship hierarchy between Test Suite(s), Test Case(s), Test Step(s), Command(s), and Comment(s) is shown in Figure 5.4.

Each Test Suite must have one and can have more than one Test Case. Each Test Case must have one and can have more than one Test Step. That said, a Test Case can be part of multiple Test Suites. A Test Step must have one Command or Comment.

Although allowing a Test Case to be in multiple Test Suites may seem confusing, it does aid managing and re-using of Test Cases. This is achieved by ensuring any changes you make in a Test Case would be reflected in each Test Suite that Test Case belongs to. This is the reason for being able to Save both a Test Case and also a Test Suite.

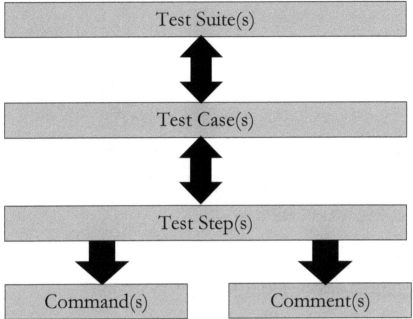

Figure 5.4. The relationship hierarchy between Test Suite(s), Test Case(s), Test Step(s), Command(s), and Comment(s).

5.5 Relationship Information

It is worth noting that if you save a Test Case that is used in multiple Test Suites, whenever you change (and re-save) that Test Case, the change you have made is reflected in each Test Suite that uses that Test Case.

Equally, any changes to a Test Step that is used in a Test Case which is in multiple Test Suites, when altered will update in each Test Case and in each Test Suite.

Chapter

6

Chapter 6: **Your first recording using Selenium IDE**

We now go step-by-step through your first recording using Selenium IDE.

Although it has taken six chapters to get here, we are finally at the point of starting to record using Selenium IDE. The first recording will be a simple recording, but will be the basis which is built-upon in future chapters (Chapter 7 and Chapter8).

In this chapter we will complete the following:

- Create a simple recording in Selenium IDE.
- Identify the steps necessary to complete a recording in Selenium IDE.
- Create a foundation on which we will build further recordings.

Although the recording in this chapter are very simple it will give you the necessary steps to create your own recording. **It is strongly recommended that you not only follow the steps in this chapter but create further recordings, so as to ensure you fully digest the information, presented in this chapter.**

6.1 First Recording - Test Scenario

Let's first set-out the Test Scenario that we will be using for our first recording:

- Test Scenario:
  Search Google for the BBC Weather site and load it.

Now let's break that down into a series of Test Cases:-

- Test Cases:

1. *Load Google Website.*
2. *Enter "BBC Weather" into the Search Textbox.*
3. *Click the Search Button.*
4. *Click on the "BBC Weather" Hyperlink.*

6.2 First Recording – Step-by-Step

Now let's start the recording. Load Firefox, and open Selenium IDE. Now click the Record Button (as shown in Figure 6.1). Now in the main Firefox URL enter the URL **www.google.co.uk** and press the Enter key (as shown in Figure 6.2). This should make three things happen:-

1. The Base URL textbox in the Selenium IDE Dialog has the value (as shown in Figure 6.3): https://www.google.co.uk/
2. Selenium IDE is in Record mode, recording your interactions.
3. Firefox is showing the Google Website.

Figure 6.1. The **Recording** Button.

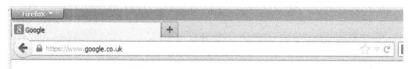

Figure 6.2. The **Firefox URL** Textbox with the URL https://www.google.co.uk entered

Figure 6.3. The **Base URL** Textbox with the URL https://www.google.co.uk shown.

Now on the Firefox session, in the Google Search Textbox enter "BBC Weather" (as shown in Figure 6.4). Next go back to the Selenium IDE and confirm that the Table element of the Test Step Pane is showing the recording information (as shown in Figure 6.5).

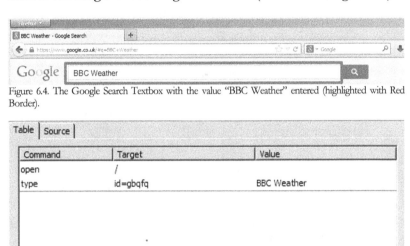

Figure 6.4. The Google Search Textbox with the value "BBC Weather" entered (highlighted with Red Border).

Figure 6.5. The Table Element of the **Test Step** Pane, which shows the recording so far.

Now it is time to click the Search Button on the Google Web Page in Firefox (as shown in Figure 6.6). Next go back to the Selenium IDE and confirm that the Table element of the Test Step Pane is showing the recording information (as shown in Figure 6.7).

Figure 6.6. The Google Search Button to click (highlighted with Red Border).

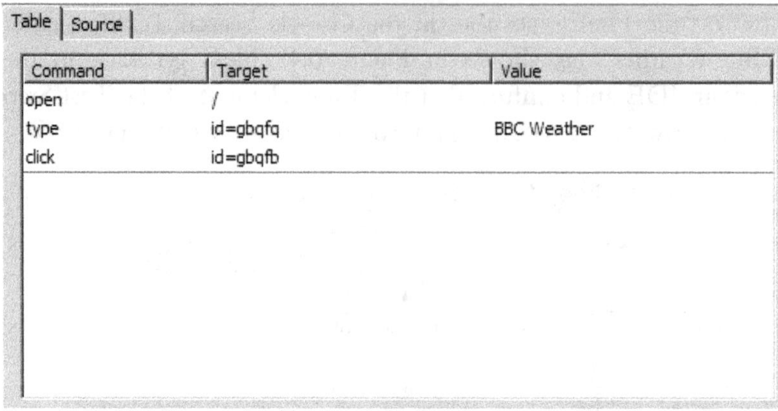

Table | Source

Command	Target	Value
open	/	
type	id=gbqfq	BBC Weather
click	id=gbqfb	

Figure 6.7. The Table Element of the **Test Step** Pane, which shows the recording so far.

Now let's go and click the "BBC Weather" Hyperlink shown on the Google Web Page in Firefox (as shown in Figure 6.8). Again, go back to the Selenium IDE and confirm that the Table element of the Test Step Pane is showing the recording information (as shown in Figure 6.9).

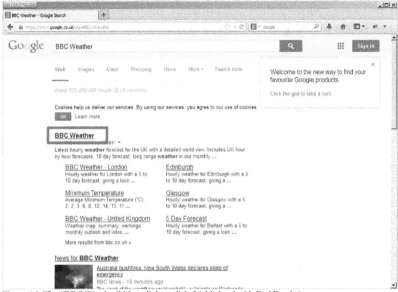

Figure 6.8. The "BBC Weather" Hyperlink to click (highlighted with Red Border).

Command	Target	Value
open	/	
type	id=gbqfq	BBC Weather
click	id=gbqfb	
clickAndWait	css=em	

Figure 6.9. The Table Element of the **Test Step** Pane, which shows the recording so far.

Now click the Recording Button in the Selenium IDE Dialog (Figure 6.1) to stop the Recording.

If you have followed the steps correctly, the Test Step Commands in your first recording, should be as in Figure 6.10.

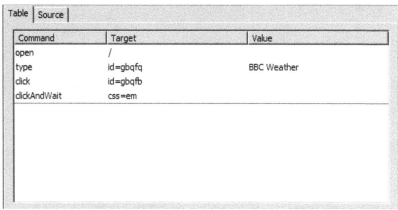

Figure 6.10. The **Test Step** Commands.

6.3 First Recording – Analysis

Let's go through the Test Step Commands. The first Command (shown in Figure 6.11) is the **Open** Command which is used to open a URL in a Web Browser, notice that the Target has the value "/" this is because we opened the URL (https://www.google.co.uk) in Firefox and this URL becomes the Base URL (Figure 6.3).

So basically, the first Command opens a Web Browser and adds the value (Target) "/" to the Base URL (https://www.google.co.uk) and will thus open the Web Browser to the following URL:

- https://www.google.co.uk/

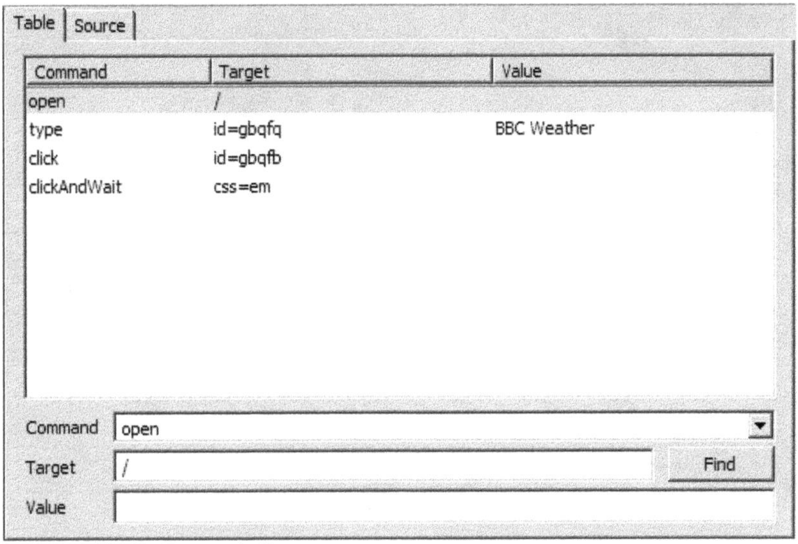

Figure 6.11. The first Command - **Open**.

The second command is **Type** (as shown in Figure 6.12), which is used to enter a value into an object (for example a textbox, input, etc.), in this example it is going to type the value "**BBC Weather**" (from the Value parameter) into the object with the **id** of **gbqfq** (**id=gbqfq** from the Target parameter). In reality this is the step which puts the value "BBC Weather" into the Google Search Textbox.

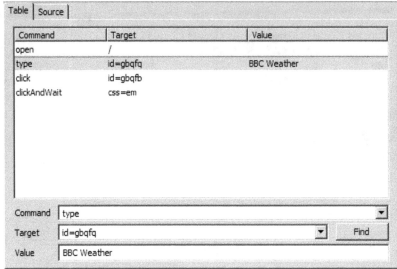

Figure 6.12. The second Command - **Type**.

The third command is **Click** (as shown in Figure 6.13), which is used to click on an object (button, checkbox, hyperlink, etc.), in this example the command is going to click on the object with the **id** of **gbqfb** (**id=gbqfb** from the Target parameter). So it is going to click on the Google Search Button.

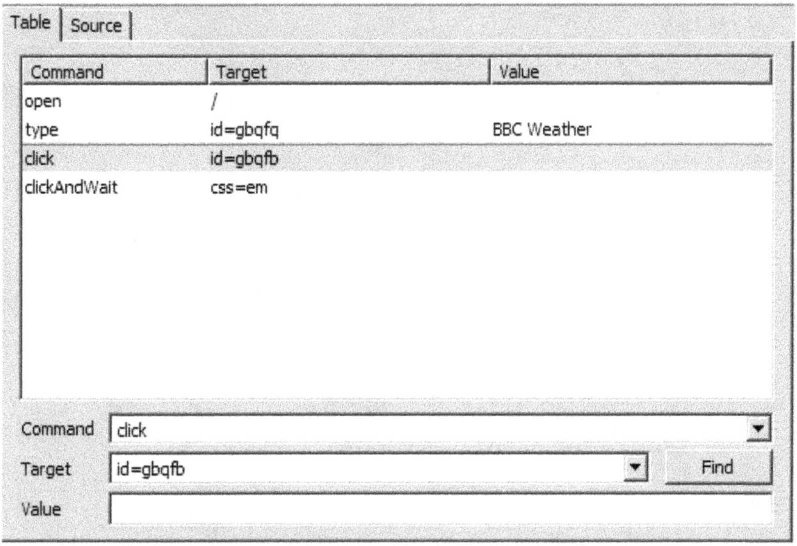

| Table | Source |

Command	Target	Value
open	/	
type	id=gbqfq	BBC Weather
click	id=gbqfb	
clickAndWait	css=em	

Command	click
Target	id=gbqfb
Value	

Find

Figure 6.13. The third Command - **Click**.

Finally, the fourth command is **ClickAndWait** (as shown in Figure 6.14), which is used to click on an object (button, checkbox, hyperlink, etc.) and then waits for the Web Page to load before completing. In this example, the command is going to click on the object with the **css** of **em** (**css=em** from the Target parameter) and then wait for the page to load). In reality, this is the step which clicks on the BBC Weather Hyperlink in the Google Search Results (Figure 6.8).

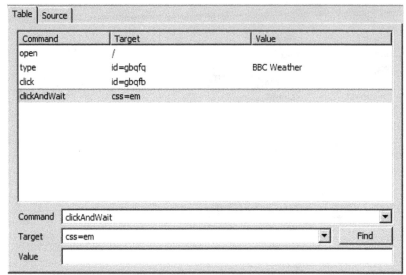

Figure 6.14. The four Command - **ClickAndWait**.

Now play-back the recording to confirm it is working as expected (use the Play Entire Test Suite Button – Section 4.4.3). You may need to slow-down the play-back speed (see Section 4.4.2). Once you have confirm the recording is working, please save it (see Section 4.3.1).

 If you encounter problems while performing the play-back, for instance elements not being found, it is most likely going to be that the play-back speed is too fast, slow down the play-back speed (see Section 4.4.2) to see if this resolves the problem.

6.4 Second Recording - Test Scenario

Let's set our Test Scenario that we will be recording for our second recording:

• Test Scenario:
  Load Google, confirm it has loaded, Search Google for the BBC Sport site and load it, then confirm the BBC Sport page has loaded.

Now let's break that down into a series of Test Cases:-

- Test Cases:

    1. *Load Google Website.*
    2. *Confirm the Google Website has loaded.*
    3. *Enter "BBC Sport" into the Search Textbox.*
    4. *Click the Search Button.*
    5. *Click on the "Home - BBC Sport" Hyperlink.*
    6. *Confirm the BBC Sport Website has loaded.*

Although the Second Recording is very similar to the First Recording (Sections 6.1 through 6.3), it is more complex and introduces the concept of validating the page has loaded, something that is incredibly important in Automated UI Testing.

6.5   Second Recording – Step-by-Step

Now let's start the recording. Load Firefox, and open Selenium IDE. Now click the Record Button (as shown in Figure 6.15). Now in the main Firefox URL enter the URL www.google.co.uk and press the Enter key (as shown in Figure 6.16). This should make three things happen:-

1. The Base URL textbox in the Selenium IDE Dialog has the value (as shown in Figure 6.17): https://www.google.co.uk/
2. Selenium IDE is in Record mode, recording your interactions.
3. Firefox is showing the Google Website.

Figure 6.15. The **Recording** Button.

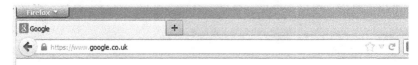

Figure 6.16. The **Firefox URL** Textbox with the URL https://www.google.co.uk entered

Figure 6.17. The **Base URL** Textbox with the URL https://www.google.co.uk shown.

Now on the Firefox session, we need to confirm that the Google Web Page has loaded, we are going to do this by confirming that the "Google" Image is being shown (see Figure 6.18). Although this is an adequate approach for this example, in the real-world the Google Image changes regularly so this is a very bad object to use to confirm the Web Page has loaded, as when the Image changes the Recording may break.

You need to be very careful when using an object being visible to determine whether a Web Page has loaded, as if that object changes the recording will stop working. Only use objects you know will not change (or are highly unlikely to change, e.g. Forms, Panes, framework objects, etc.)

Figure 6.18. The **Google** Image object we will validate is visible (shown with Red Border).

Now Right-Hand Click on the "**Google**" Image, this will load the Quick Access Menu (as shown in Figure 6.19). On the Quick Access Menu the bottom three items (**open /**, **verify**, and **Show All Available Commands**) relate to Selenium IDE. Now select **Show All Available Commands** to show all the available Selenium IDE Commands for this object (as shown in Figure 6.20).

Figure 6.19. The Quick Access Menu (loaded by Right-Hand Mouse Clicking an object).

Figure 6.20. The **Show All Available Commands** sub-menu of the Quick Access Menu (loaded by Right-Hand Mouse Clicking an object and selecting the Show All Available Commands Menu Item).

Now select **Show All Available Commands** > **Verify Element Present ID = hplogo** (as shown in Figure 6.21). Next go back to the Selenium IDE and confirm that the Table element of the Test Step Pane is showing the recording information (as shown in Figure 6.22).

Figure 6.21. The **Show All Available Commands** > **Verify Element Present** Menu Item.

Command	Target	Value
open	/	
verifyElementPresent	id=hplogo	

Table | Source

Figure 6.22. The Table Element of the **Test Step** Pane, which shows the recording so far.

Now in the Google Search Textbox enter "BBC Sport" (as shown in Figure 6.23). Next go back to the Selenium IDE and confirm that the Table element of the Test Step Pane is showing the recording information (as shown in Figure 6.24).

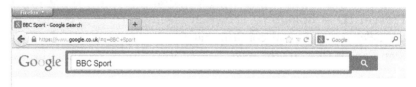

Figure 6.23. The Google Search Textbox with "BBC Sport" entered (shown with Red Border).

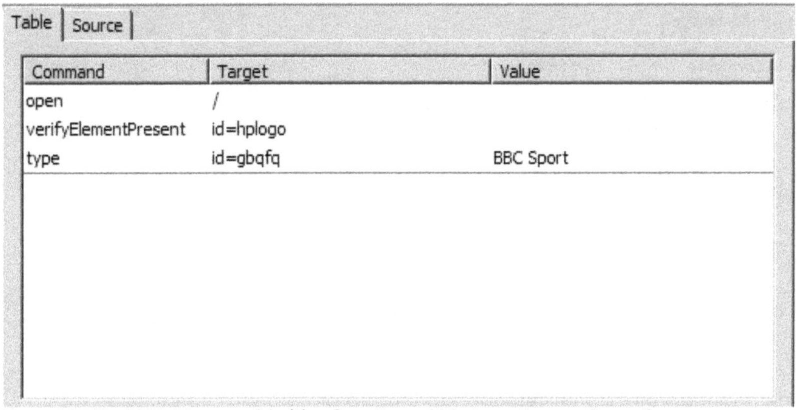

Table
Source
Command
Target
Value
open
/
verifyElementPresent
id=hplogo
type
id=gbqfq
BBC Sport

Figure 6.24. The Table Element of the **Test Step** Pane, which shows the recording so far.

Now it is time to click the Search Button on the Google Website in Firefox (as shown in Figure 6.25). Next go back to the Selenium IDE and confirm that the Table element of the Test Step Pane is showing the recording information (as shown in Figure 6.26).

Firefox
BBC Sport - Google Search
https://www.google.co.uk/#q=BBC+Sport
Google
Google
BBC Sport

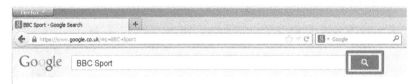

Figure 6.25. The Google Search Button (shown with Red Border).

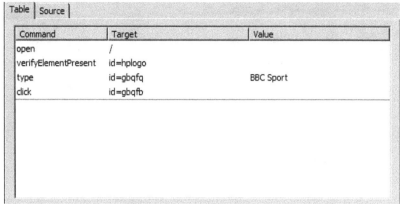

Figure 6.26. The Table Element of the **Test Step** Pane, which shows the recording so far.

Now let's go and click the "Homepage - BBC Sport" Hyperlink shown on the Google Website in Firefox (as shown in Figure 6.27). Again, go back to the Selenium IDE and confirm that the Table element of the Test Step Pane is showing the recording information (as shown in Figure 6.28).

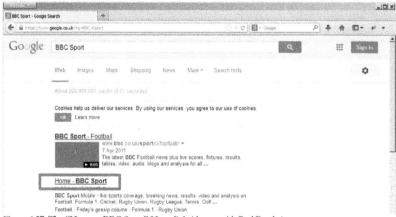

Figure 6.27. The "Home – BBC Sport" Hyperlink (shown with Red Border).

Table	Source

Command	Target	Value
open	/	
verifyElementPresent	id=hplogo	
type	id=gbqfq	BBC Sport
click	id=gbqfb	
clickAndWait	//ol[@id='rso']/li[2]/div/h3/a/em	

Figure 6.28. The Table Element of the **Test Step** Pane, which shows the recording so far.

Now on the Firefox session, we need to confirm that the BBC Sport Web Page has loaded, we are going to do this by confirming that the "Sport" Image is being shown (see Figure 6.29). Although this is an adequate approach for this example, in the real-world the BBC Sport Image changes regularly so this is a very bad object to use to confirm the Web Page has loaded, as when the Image changes the Recording will break.

You need to be very careful when using an object being visible to determine whether a Web Page has loaded, as if that Object changes the Recording will stop working. Only use objects you know will not change (or are highly unlikely to change, e.g. Forms, Panes, framework objects, etc.)

Now Right-Hand Click on the "**Sport**" Image, this will load the Quick Access Menu (as shown in Figure 6.19). On the Quick Access Menu select **Show All Available Commands > Verify Element Present CSS = span.logo** (as shown in Figure 6.30). Next go back to the Selenium IDE and confirm that the Table element of the Test Step Pane is showing the recording information (as shown in Figure 6.31).

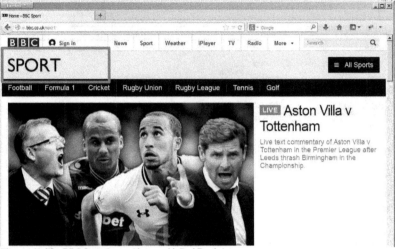

Figure 6.29. The BBC Sport Image (shown with Red Border).

Figure 6.30. The **Show All Available Commands > Verify Element** Present CSS = span.logo (available via Right-Hand Mouse Clicking the BBC Sport Image).

Command	Target	Value
open	/	
verifyElementPresent	id=hplogo	
type	id=gbqfq	BBC Sport
click	id=gbqfb	
clickAndWait	//ol[@id='rso']/li[2]/div/h3/a/em	
verifyElementPresent	css=span.logo	

Table | Source |

Figure 6.31. The Table Element of the **Test Step** Pane, which shows the recording so far.

Now click the Recording Button in the Selenium IDE Dialog (Figure 6.1) to stop the Recording.

If you have followed the steps correctly, the Test Step Commands in your second recording, should be as in Figure 6.32.

Command	Target	Value
open	/	
verifyElementPresent	id=hplogo	
type	id=gbqfq	BBC Sport
click	id=gbqfb	
clickAndWait	//ol[@id='rso']/li[2]/div/h3/a/em	
verifyElementPresent	css=span.logo	

Table | Source |

Figure 6.32. The **Test Step** Commands of our Second Recording.

6.6 Second Recording – Analysis

Let's go through the Test Step Commands. The first command (shown in Figure 6.32) is the **Open** Command which is used to open a URL in a Web Browser, notice that the Target has the value "**/**" this is because we opened the URL (https://www.google.co.uk) in Firefox and became the Base URL (Figure 6.3). So basically, the first Command opens a Web Browser and adds the value (Target) "**/**" to the Base URL (https://www.google.co.uk) and will thus open the Web Browser to the following URL:

- https://www.google.co.uk/

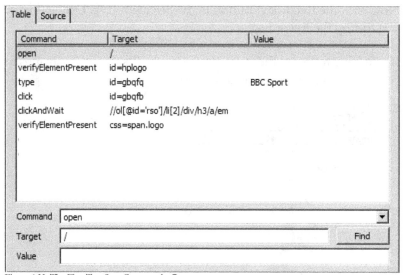

Figure 6.33. The First Test Step Command - **Open**.

The second command is **VerifyElementPresent** (as shown in Figure 6.34), which is used to confirm that an object on the Web Page is visible (in this example the object with the **id** of **hplogo** – **id=hplogo** in the Target Column), this is the "Google" Image.

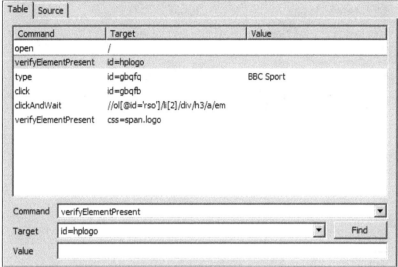

Command	Target	Value
open	/	
verifyElementPresent	id=hplogo	
type	id=gbqfq	BBC Sport
click	id=gbqfb	
clickAndWait	//ol[@id='rso']/li[2]/div/h3/a/em	
verifyElementPresent	css=span.logo	

Command: verifyElementPresent

Target: id=hplogo   Find

Value:

Figure 6.34. The Second Test Step Command – **Verify Element Present**.

The third command **Type** (as shown in Figure 6.35), which is used to set the value of an object (textbox, input, etc.) in this example it is going to type the value "**BBC Sport**" (from the Value parameter) into the object with the **id** of **gbqfq** (**id=gbqfq** from the Target parameter). In reality this is the step which puts the value "BBC Sport" into the Google Search Textbox.

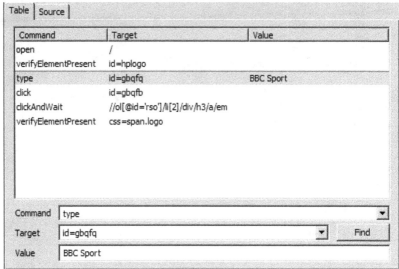

Figure 6.35. The Third Test Step Command - **Type**.

The fourth command is **Click** (as shown in Figure 6.36), which is used to click on an object (button, checkbox, hyperlink, etc.), in this example the command is going to click on the object with the **id** of **gbqfb** (**id=gbqfb** from the Target parameter). So it is going to click on the Google Search Button.

The fifth command is **ClickAndWait** (as shown in Figure 6.37), which is used to click on an object (button, checkbox, hyperlink, etc.) and then wait for the Web Page to load, in this example the command is going to click on the object searching for an **id** of **'rso'** and then the second element below it (**//ol[@id='rso']/li[2]/div/h3/a/em** from the Target parameter). So it is going to click on the Homepage - BBC Sport Hyperlink in the Google Search Results (Figure 6.27).

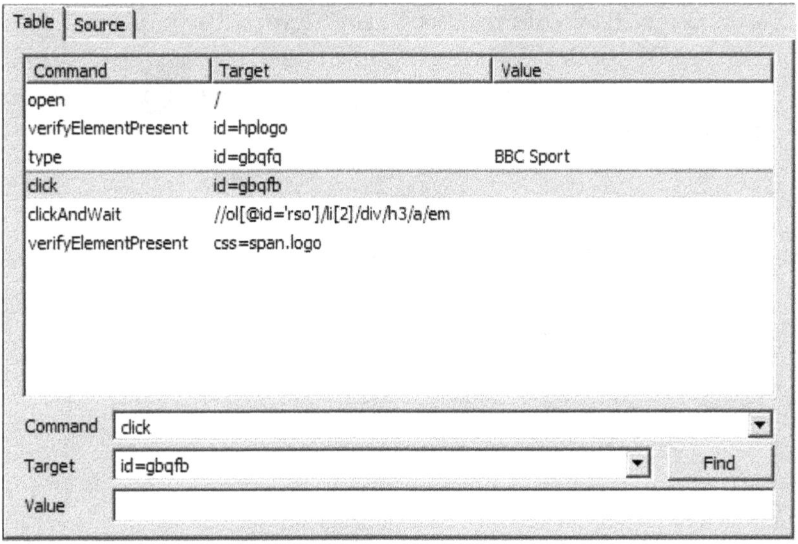

| Table | Source |

Command	Target	Value
open	/	
verifyElementPresent	id=hplogo	
type	id=gbqfq	BBC Sport
click	id=gbqfb	
clickAndWait	//ol[@id='rso']/li[2]/div/h3/a/em	
verifyElementPresent	css=span.logo	

Command: click

Target: id=gbqfb   [Find]

Value:

Figure 6.36. The Fourth Test Step Command - **Click.**

| Table | Source |

Command	Target	Value
open	/	
verifyElementPresent	id=hplogo	
type	id=gbqfq	BBC Sport
click	id=gbqfb	
clickAndWait	//ol[@id='rso']/li[2]/div/h3/a/em	
verifyElementPresent	css=span.logo	

Command: clickAndWait

Target: //ol[@id='rso']/li[2]/div/h3/a/em   [Find]

Value:

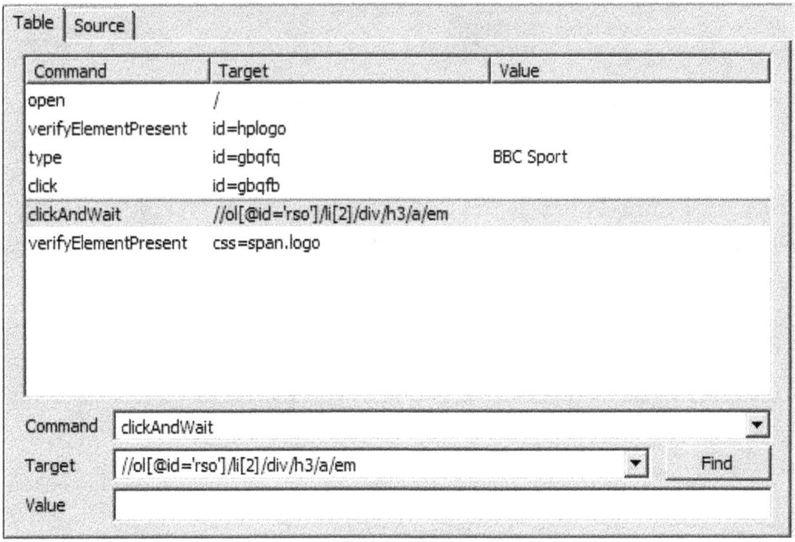

Figure 6.37. The Fifth Test Step Command - **ClickAndWait.**

The sixth and final command is **VerifyElementPresent** (as shown in Figure 6.38), which is used to confirm that an object on the Web Page is visible (in this example the object with the **css** of **span.logo** – **css=span.logo** in the Target Column), this is the "Sport" Image.

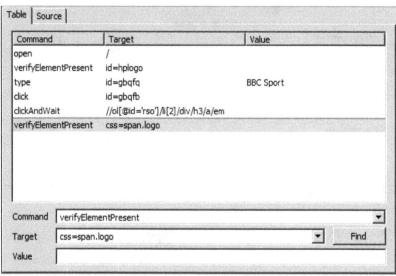

Figure 6.38. The Sixth Test Step Command - **VerifyElementPresent**.

Now playback the recording to confirm it is working as expected (use the Play Entire Test Suite Button – Section 4.4.3). You may need to slow-down the play-back speed (see Section 4.4.2). Once you have confirm the recording is working, please save it (see Section 4.3.1).

> If you encounter problems while performing the play-back, for instance elements not being found, it is most likely going to be that the play-back speed is too fast, slow down the play-back speed (see Section 4.4.2) to see if this resolves the problem.

6.7 Task Test Scenarios

Let's set you some Test Scenarios to record for yourself:

• Test Scenario 1:

Load Google, Search Google for the Amazon site and load it, then confirm the Amazon page has loaded.

- Test Scenario 2:
  Load Google, Search Google for the Ebay site and load it, then confirm the Amazon page has loaded.

- Test Scenario 3:
  Load Google, Search Google for the Amazon site and load it, then confirm the Amazon page has loaded. Perform a search in Amazon in Film & TV Department for the film Avatar. Select the second item returned and load it. Confirm the page loads.

- Test Scenario 4:
  Load the BBC Website (www.bbc.co.uk), and click on the Radio Menu.

- Test Scenario 5:
  Load the BBC Website (www.bbc.co.uk), click on the Radio Menu, and click on the What's On Button.

- Test Scenario 6:
  Load the BBC Website (www.bbc.co.uk), and use the Search Box to search for Sport. Click the third returned item.

Although this may seem like overkill, it is highly recommended that you complete these recordings to gain more experience of recording using Selenium IDE.

Chapter 7: Replaying your recordings using Selenium IDE

We now go step-by-step through replaying your recordings using Selenium IDE.

I n Chapter 6, we created our first few recording using Selenium

IDE, now in this Chapter we will learn about playing-back recordings. This Chapter will cover the following:-

- How to Play-back a Recording.
- How to Speed-up or Slow-down the Play-back.
- How to Play-back all Test Cases.
- How to Play-back a specific Test Case.
- How to Pause and Resume the Play-back.
- How to Step through a Play-back.
- How to Execute a single Command.

Although the recording used in this chapter is very simple it will give you the necessary knowledge to use the play-back features. **As ever it is worth spending time using the play-back features to gain further experience and aid your learning.**

7.1 Playing back your first recording

Let's play-back our first recording. The easiest way to do this is to click on the **Play Entire Test Suite** Button (Figure 7.1) or Actions > Play Entire Test Suite Menu Item (Figure 7.2).

Figure 7.1. The **Play Entire Test Suite** Button.

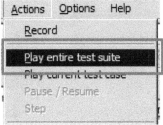

Figure 7.2. The **Actions > Play Entire Test Suite** Menu Item (highlighted with Red Border).

This will play-back the recording at the default speed (Fastest Speed of 0). This should be fine for most usage but can occasionally cause problems as the play-back could try to run a command before the element is available to be acted on. Section 7.2, talks you through speeding-up the Play-back and Section 7.3, talks you through slowing-down the Play-back.

7.2 Speeding-up Play-back

The purpose of Automated Testing is obviously to do the same amount of testing quicker than can be done manually. Therefore, it would be ideal to run the play-back as fast as is possible. To accommodate this Selenium IDE allows you to use the Play-back **Speed** Slider (Figure 7.3) to change the Play-back Speed.

Figure 7.3. The **Play-back Speed** Slider.

By moving the Green circle towards the left (where it shows "Fast") it will run the play-back faster (as shown in Figure 7.4), moving it to the right (where it shows "Slow") will slow-down the play-back speed (as shown in Figure 7.5). Whilst moving the Green circle to the middle will give a medium play-back speed (as shown in Figure 7.6).

Figure 7.4. The fastest play-back speed on the **Speed** Slider.

Figure 7.5. The slowest play-back speed on the **Speed** Slider.

Figure 7.6. The middle play-back speed on the **Speed** Slider.

So to increase the play-back speed you can either move the Play-back Speed Slider towards "Fast" (as shown in Figure 7.4) or use the Actions > Fastest (0) Menu Item (Figure 7.7) or Actions > Faster (-) Menu Item (Figure 7.8).

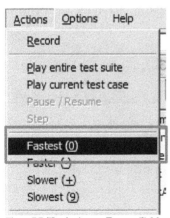
Figure 7.7. The **Actions > Fastest (0)** Menu Item (highlighted in Red Border).

SELENIUM BY EXAMPLE - VOLUME I: SELENIUM IDE

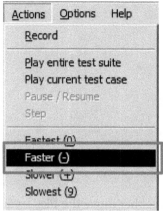

Figure 7.8. The **Actions > Faster (-)** Menu Item (highlighted in Red Border).

Be warned that if the play-back runs too fast it may encounter problems because the element the command is acting upon is not available. This is discussed in Section 7.4.

 Running your play-back too fast, means there is a risk that an element the command is being performed on is not available and thus the play-back of the recording will fail.

7.3 Slowing-down Play-back

To accommodate the ability to slow-down play-back, Selenium IDE allows you to use the Play-back Speed Slider (Figure 7.3) to change the Play-back Speed.

By moving the Green circle towards the left (where it shows "Fast") it will run the play-back faster (as shown in Figure 7.4), moving it to the right (where it shows "Slow") will slow-down the play-back speed (as shown in Figure 7.5). Whilst moving the Green circle to the middle will give a medium play-back speed (as shown in Figure 7.6).

95

So to decrease the play-back speed you can either move the Play-back Speed Slider towards "Slow" (as shown in Figure 7.5) or use the Actions > Slowest (9) Menu Item (Figure 7.9) or Actions > Slower (+) Menu Item (Figure 7.10).

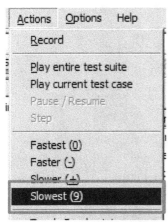

Figure 7.9. The **Actions > Slowest (9)** Menu Item (highlighted in Red Border).

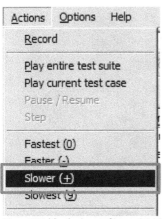

Figure 7.10. The **Actions > Slower (+)** Menu Item (highlighted in Red Border).

7.4 Play-back speed problems

It is common when running play-back of recordings at full speed, to hit problems (most notably "Element ... not found" (as shown in Figure 7.11).

Log	Reference	UI-Element	Rollup

[info] Executing: |clickAndWait | css=em | |
[error] Element css=em not found

Figure 7.11. An **Element not found** Error on the element css=em.

Firstly, let's discuss what this error is tells you, and then we can discuss why you get this error. The error is tell you that the element (object on the Web Page) – in the case of Figure 7.11 the Element **css=em** could not be found on the Web Page. The Element name relates to the Target section of the Test Steps (Figure 7.12).

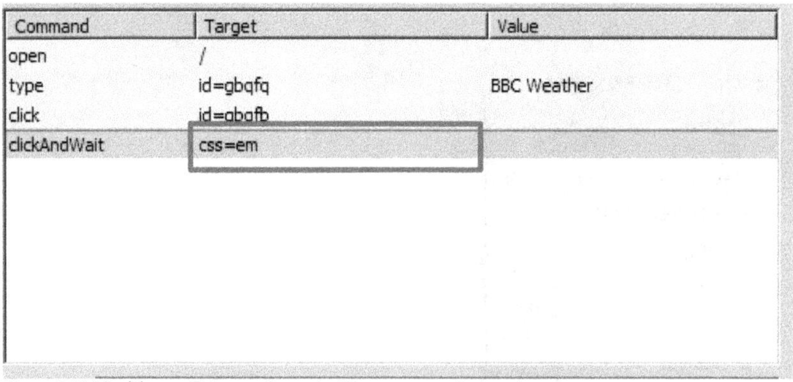

Command	Target	Value
open	/	
type	id=gbqfq	BBC Weather
click	id=gbqfb	
clickAndWait	css=em	

Figure 7.12. The **Target Column** shows the Element name (css=em).

So that is what the error is telling you. But why are you getting this error? The reason is that the play-back is so fast that the Web Page has not had enough time to load the element (css=em in this example) to be able to perform the Command **ClickAndWait** against the element.

This is a common problem to encounter, because it can take anywhere from milli-seconds to many seconds to:

- Call the Web Page (as a request)
- Get the Web Page (as a response).
- Render (load and display) the Web Page in the Browser (and populate the DOM).
- Populate the DOM for the element to be available so as to be used by Selenium IDE to run the Command.

So now we know what the error is and why it is happening, how do we prevent it from occurring? Two options exist. Firstly, to slow-down the play-back speed (see Section 7.3) or to add WaitFor… commands to ensure the element exists before the command is ran upon the element.

7.5 Play-back all Test Cases

When you perform play-back you are most likely going to use the **Play Entire Test Suite** option (Figure 7.13 shows the Button, whilst Figure 7.14 shows the Menu Item).

Figure 7.13. The **Play Entire Test Suite** Button.

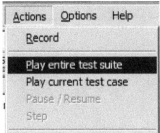

Figure 7.14. The **Actions > Play Entire Test Suite** Menu Item.

The Play Entire Test Suite option allows you to run all the Test Cases in the Test Suite. This is for when you want to run the whole Test Suite, for instance when you want to re-run the tests to actually see whether the Web Page functionality is working correctly. Each Test Case, starting from the first in the Test Case Listbox (Figure 4.4) through to the last is ran in sequence.

This option is obviously the most thorough play-back option, but will be the most time consuming to run (as each and every Test Case in the Test Suite is ran).

7.6 Play-back a specific Test Cases

When you wish to run just one of your Test Cases from the Test Case Listbox (Figure 4.4), you need to firstly select the Test Case (as shown in Figure 7.15), then select the **Play Current Test Case** option (Figure 7.16 shows the Button, whilst Figure 7.17 shows the Menu Item).

The Play Current Test Case option is used to run part of the Test Suite, as it will run just one of the Test Cases (the selected Test Case). This approach is particularly useful when you want to confirm specific functionality is working, or if you want to continuously re-run the selected Test Case for a specific piece of functionality on the Web Page.

Figure 7.15. The **Test Case** Listbox, showing the **Google-Search-2** Test Case selected (highlighted in Red Border).

Figure 7.16. The **Play Current Test Case** Button.

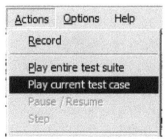

Figure 7.17. The **Actions > Play Case Test Case** Menu Item.

As a general rule-of-thumb it is best to use the Play Current Test Case (Section 7.6) when building-up a Test Suite, and to use the Play Entire Test Suite (Section 7.5) when testing functionality.

7.7 Pausing Play-back

During the play-back of a recording it is useful to be able to pause the play-back, for example if you want to ensure an object is in a usable state or if you want to manually interact with the Web Page, before continuing the play-back. To pause the play-back you need to click the **Pause / Resume** Button (when it is showing the Pause Icon - as shown in Figure 7.18) or the **Pause / Resume** Menu Item (Figure 7.19).

Figure 7.18. The **Pause / Resume** Button. (enabled to pause play-back).

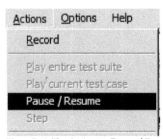

Figure 7.19. The **Actions > Pause / Resume** Menu Item.

7.8 Resuming Play-back

When the play-back of a recording is paused, to resume (continue the play-back) you need to click the **Pause / Resume** Button (when it is showing the Resume Icon - as shown in Figure 7.20) or the **Pause / Resume** Menu Item (Figure 7.21).

Figure 7.20. The **Pause / Resume** Button. (enabled to resume play-back).

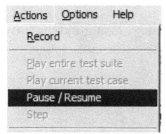

Figure 7.21. The **Actions > Pause / Resume** Menu Item.

7.9 Step through Play-back

The **Step** option (Button as shown in Figure 7.22 and Menu Item shown in Figure 7.23) is an easy way to "step" Command by Command/Test Case by Test Case through the entire Test Suite. The Step option will allow you to run one Command at a time, so a Command is executed and then Selenium IDE waits for you press the Step Button again.

Figure 7.22. The **Step** Button.

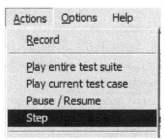

Figure 7.23. The **Actions > Step** Menu Item.

The Step option is very useful to run just one Command, either when you are trying to debug the Test Steps of a Test Case or if you want to just play-back that single Command to test a specific part of functionality of a Web Page.

Once the Step option has been ran, so the single Command has been played-back, you can then use any of the following options to continue:

- **Play Entire Test Suite** (Section 7.5): to play the whole of the Test Suite from the start.
- **Play Current Test Case** (Section 7.6): to play the rest of the selected Test Case.
- **Resume** (Section 7.8): to continue playing-back from the next Command, of the currently selected Test Case.
- **Step** (Section 7.9): to play-back the next Command of the selected Test Case.
- **Execute** (Section 10): just play-back the selected Command.

As well as speeding-up or slowing-down the play-back of the recording (Section 7.2 and Section 7.3).

7.10 Execute this Command

The option to execute just a single Command is available via the **Execute This Command** Menu Item (Figure 7.24). This option allows you to execute just the selected Command of the selected Test Case in isolation. This feature is useful if you wanted to play-back just one Command at a time. The Execute This Command is commonly used to play-back a Command from your recording, for example to run a Command and view the results before continuing.

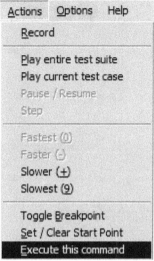

Figure 7.24. The **Actions > Execute This Command** Menu Item.

7.11 Review of Play-back options

The various play-back options such as: setting speed of play-back (Sections 7.2 and 7.3); playing the entire Test Suite (Section 7.5); playing just the current Test Case (Section 7.6); pausing and resuming play-back (Sections 7.7 and 7.8); stepping through the Commands (Section 7.9); or executing just a single Command (Section 7.10), can all be used to either re-run the recording to test the functionality of the Web Page or to debug the Command or Test Case (if you are finding it is producing incorrect or unexpected results.

Chapter

8

Chapter 8: More advanced recordings

We now introduce some of the more advanced techniques available in Selenium IDE.

I n this chapter, we expand on the recording examples of Chapter

6, introducing some new features of Selenium IDE, which will help you to create more useful and robust automation test. The Chapter will cover the following:-

- Verify Commands.
- Assert Commands.
- "AndWait" Commands.
- Manually adding Commands.
- Manually adding Comments.
- Matching Text Patterns.

8.1 Introduction

In this chapter we will building a more advanced Test Case, we will be manually adding all the commands to the Test Step Pane, as this chapter is concerned with creating more advanced Test Cases.

8.2 Test Case - Basis

For the purpose of this chapter, we will be using the following Test Case as a basis, upon which we add various options. Figure 8.1 shows the basic Test Case (the first recording from Chapter 6).

Command	Target	Value
open	/	
type	id=gbqfq	BBC Weather
click	id=gbqfb	
clickAndWait	css=em	

Figure 8.1. The Test Case that will be the basis for this chapter.

8.3 Test Case – Additions

During the course of this Chapter we will add the following items to the Test Case basis (shown in Figure 8.1). Each addition will add value to the Test Case, in terms of either improving the quality of testing being performed by the Test Case or in-terms of ensuring the Test Case is more robust.

The following additions will be made to the Test Case:

- Asserting the Google Web Page has loaded.
- Verifying that the Search Textbox is available on the Google Web Page.
- "AndWait" Commands.
- Comments.

8.4 Verify versus Assert Commands

Before we go into adding Verify and Assert Commands into our Test Case, it is important to understand the difference between the Verify and the Assert Commands.

Both the Verify and the Assert Commands are used to check to see if an element exists, for example both can be used to confirm whether a Textbox exists on the Web Page.

The main difference between using a Verify Command and a Assert Command is that both will fail the Test Step if the element is not there, but the Verify Command will allow the Test Case to continue, whilst the Assert Command will stop the Test Case.

- **Verify** – When the Command fails the Test Case still continues.
- **Assert** – When the Command fails the Test Case stops.

The next question is when should you use Verify Commands and when should you use Assert Commands? As a rule-of-thumb, you should use Assert Commands to confirm that the Web Page has loaded (as if the Web Page does not load, there is no value in continuing the Test Case). You should use the Verify Commands to confirm Web Page elements are loaded (as if the element has not loaded it could be a software bug, so it is best to allow the Test Case to continue).

8.5 Adding Assert Commands

Let's start by adding an **AssertTitle** Command. Select the second Test Step (**type** Command) in the Test Case, and then select **Edit > Insert New Command** Menu Item, this should add a blank Test Step at the beginning of the Test Case (as shown in Figure 8.2).

Command	Target	Value
open	/	
type	id=gbqfq	BBC Weather
click	id=gbqfb	
clickAndWait	css=em	

Figure 8.2. The blank Command in the Test Case (highlighted with Red Border).

Now we are going to populate the values for the Command:-

- Command = **assertTitle**
- Target = **Google**
- Value = <leave blank>

If you have entered the values, correctly it should look like Figure 8.3.

Command	Target	Value
open	/	
assertTitle	Google	
type	id=gbqfq	BBC Weather
click	id=gbqfb	
clickAndWait	css=em	

Figure 8.3. The added **Test Step** (**AssertTitle**), highlighted in Red Border.

The AssertTitle Command added in Figure 8.3 will confirm that the Title of Window loaded by the Open Command has the value "Google", if it does not it will fail (and stop the Test Case at that point). If the value does match "Google" it will pass. Play-back the recording and confirm this is ok.

Below are some tasks for you to complete:

- Play-back the recording and confirm the play-back passes.
- Change the Target to "**Googlee**" and confirm the play-back fails.
- Change the Target to "**Goog***" and confirm the play-back passes.

8.6 Adding Verify Commands

Let's start by adding a **VerifyElementPresent** Command. Select the third Test Step (**type** Command) in the Test Case, and then select **Edit > Insert New Command** Menu Item, this should add a blank Test Step at the beginning of the Test Case (as shown in Figure 8.4).

Command	Target	Value
open	/	
assertTitle	Google	
type	id=gbqfq	BBC Weather
click	id=gbqfb	
clickAndWait	css=em	

Figure 8.4. The Test Case that with the new Command.

Now we are going to populate the values for the Command:-

- Command   = **verifyElementPresent**
- Target   = **id=gs_tti0**
- Value   = <leave blank>

If you have entered the values, correctly it should look like Figure 8.5.

Command	Target	Value
open	/	
assertTitle	Google	
verifyElementPresent	id=gs_tti0	
type	id=gbqfq	BBC Weather
click	id=gbqfb	
clickAndWait	css=em	

Figure 8.5. The added **Test Step** (**VerifyElementPresent**), highlighted in Red Border.

Below are some tasks for you to complete:

- Play-back the recording and confirm the play-back passes.
- Change the Target to "**id=gs_tti01**" and confirm the play-back fails.
- Change the Target to "**id=gs_tt***" and confirm the play-back fails.

8.7 Adding "AndWait" Commands

Let's add a **WaitForPageToLoad** Command. Select the last Test Step (**clickAndWait** Command) in the Test Case, and then select **Edit > Insert New Command** Menu Item, this should add a blank Test Step in the Test Case (as shown in Figure 8.6).

Command	Target	Value
open	/	
assertTitle	Google	
verifyElementPresent	id=gs_tti0	
type	id=gbqfq	BBC Weather
click	id=gbqfb	
clickAndWait	css=em	

Figure 8.6. The Test Case that with the new Command.

Now we are going to populate the values for the Command:-

- Command   = **waitForPageToLoad**
- Target   = \<leave blank\>
- Value   = \<leave blank\>

If you have entered the values, correctly it should look like Figure 8.7.

Command	Target	Value
open	/	
assertTitle	Google	
verifyElementPresent	id=gs_tti0	
type	id=gbqfq	BBC Weather
click	id=gbqfb	
clickAndWait	css=em	
waitForPageToLoad		

Figure 8.7. The added **Test Step** (**WaitForPageToLoad**), highlighted in Red Border.

8.8 Adding Comments

Let's add a **Comment**. Select the first Test Step (**Open** Command) in the Test Case, and then select **Edit > Insert New Comment** Menu Item, this should add a blank Test Step in the Test Case (as shown in Figure 8.8).

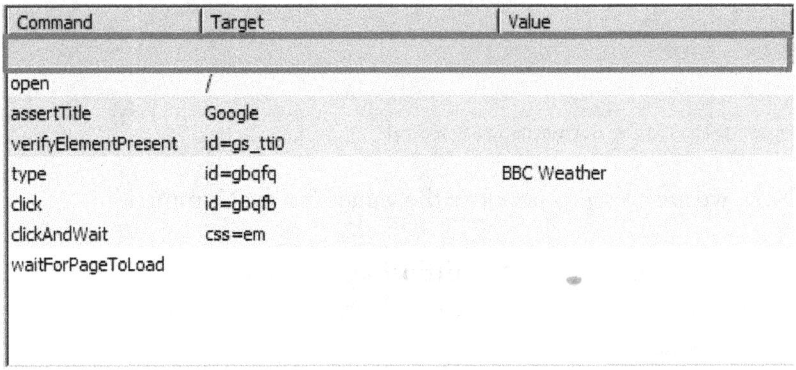

Command	Target	Value
open	/	
assertTitle	Google	
verifyElementPresent	id=gs_tti0	
type	id=gbqfq	BBC Weather
click	id=gbqfb	
clickAndWait	css=em	
waitForPageToLoad		

Figure 8.8. The Test Case that with the new Comment.

Now we are going to populate the values for the Command:-

- Command   = **This Is My Comment.**

If you have entered the values, correctly it should look like Figure 8.9.

Command	Target	Value
This Is My Comment.		
open	/	
assertTitle	Google	
verifyElementPresent	id=gs_tti0	
type	id=gbqfq	BBC Weather
click	id=gbqfb	
clickAndWait	css=em	
waitForPageToLoad		

Figure 8.9. The added **Test Step** (**Comment**), highlighted in Red Border.

Below are some tasks for you to complete:

- Play-back the recording and confirm the play-back passes.
- Add three more comments to the Test Case.

8.9 Next Step

The next step is for you to add further Commands and Comments to the Test Case to build-up a more robust and usable Test Case. **I cannot recommend enough the need for you to spend time adding more Commands and Comments so as to re-enforce your learning from this chapter and to expand and broaden your understanding of the topics covered in this chapter.**

Chapter 9: **Exporting recordings**

We now introduce how you can export your recordings from Selenium IDE.

I n this chapter, we look at exporting recordings created in

Selenium IDE. The Chapter will cover the following:-

- How to export a Test Case.
- How to export a Test Suite.
- What Formats you can export to.
- Adding a new Format to export to.

9.1 Why export your recordings

As Selenium IDE allows you to record, play-back your recordings, and save your recordings (as both Test Cases and Test Suites), why is there a need to export these recordings?

There are several answers to the question:

- Firstly, Selenium IDE only allows recording and play-back in Mozilla Firefox, so if you wanted to run your recording in another Web Browser you would need to export it to a different version of Selenium (Selenium Remote Control or Selenium Web Driver).
- Secondly, you may want to build a framework (such as a Keyword Driven or Data Driven framework) which would require more complex coding and need Selenium RC or Selenium WebDriver).
- Thirdly, you could wish to build a large Test Script which Selenium IDE would struggle to handle.
- Fourthly, could be you may want to user features around Selenium Grid (where you can run multiple Selenium instances at the same time).

9.2 How to export a Test Case

To export a Test Case from Selenium IDE is a simple case of selecting the Test Case to export and then choosing the **Export Test Case As** Menu Item (Figure 9.1).

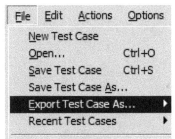

Figure 9.1. The **File > Export Test Case As** Menu Item.

The Export Test Case As Menu Item is available from the File Menu, and has a sub-menu (see Figure 9.2) which will list all of the Formats that have been setup in the Options section of Selenium IDE (see Sections 4.3.7 and 4.3.9 for further information).

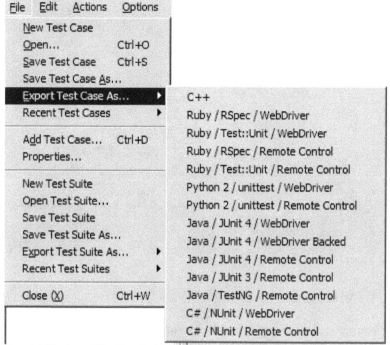

Figure 9.2. The **Export Test Case As** Sub-Menu (listing the various formats you can export a Test Case into).

Once you have selected one of the Formats from the Sub-Menu, a Save As dialog will be shown (Figure 9.3) which will allow you to select the Location and Name of the file to save the Test Case as. Once you click save it will export the Test Case in the format setup in the Options section of Selenium IDE.

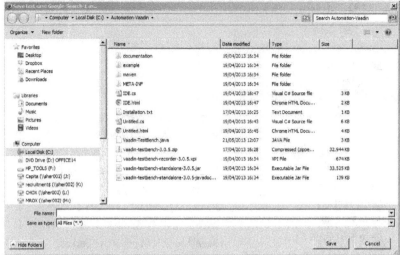

Figure 9.3. The **Save As** Dialog.

9.3 How to export a Test Suite

To export a Test Suite from Selenium IDE is a simple case of selecting the **Export Test Suite As** Menu Item (Figure 9.4).

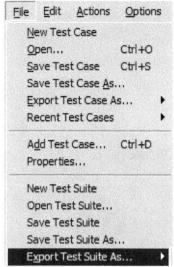

Figure 9.4. The **File > Export Test Suite As** Menu Item.

The Export Test Suite As Menu Item is available from the File Menu, and has a sub-menu (see Figure 9.5) which will list a subset of the available Formats that have been setup in the Options section of Selenium IDE (see Sections 4.3.7 and 4.3.9 for further information).

Once you have selected one of the Formats from the Sub-Menu, a Save As dialog will be shown (Figure 9.6) which will allow you to select the Location and Name of the file to save the Test Case as. Once you click save it will export the Test Case in the format setup in the Options section of Selenium IDE.

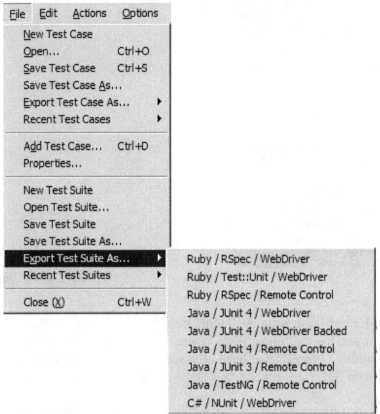

Figure 9.5 The **Export Test Suite As** Sub-Menu,)showing the available formats to export to).

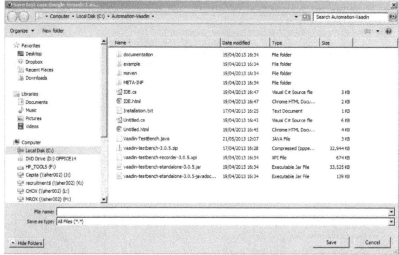

Figure 9.6. The **Save As** Dialog.

9.4 What Formats you can export to

Within the Options (Figure 9.8) section of Selenium IDE (via the
Options > Options Menu Item – Figure 9.7), there is a **Formats** Tab
(see Figure 9.9) which lists out all of the Formats that are currently
available to export to via Selenium IDE.

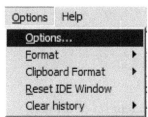

Figure 9.7. The **Options > Options** Menu Item.

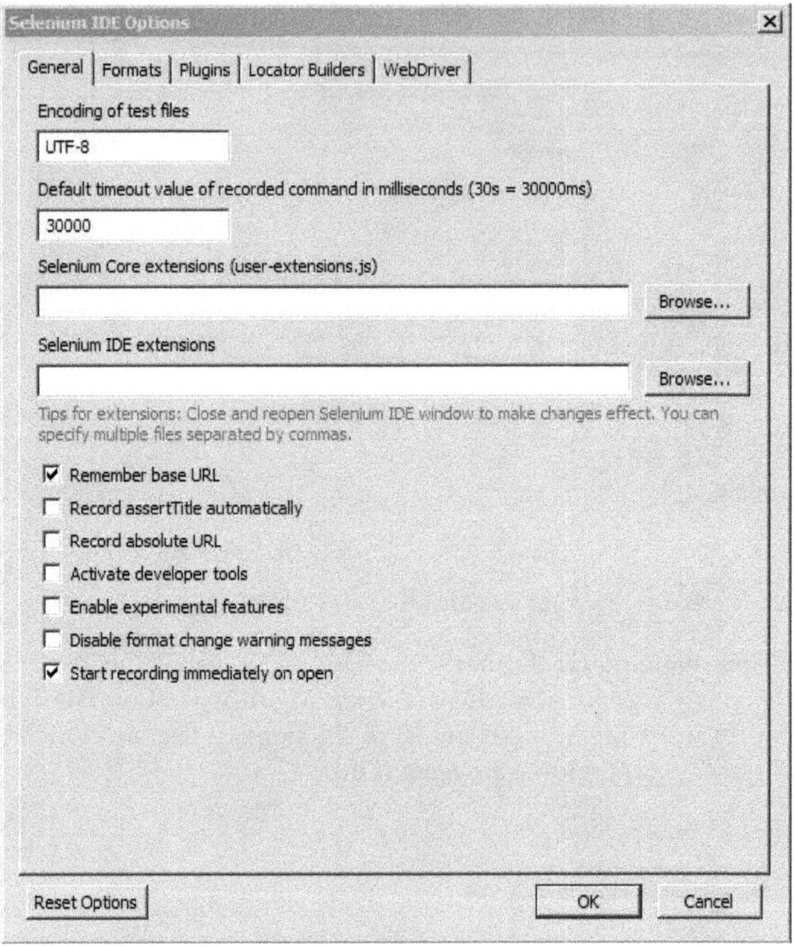

Figure 9.8. The **Options** Dialog.

Depending on the Format you will get a different set of settings, for example the settings around the **HTML** Format are shown in Figure 9.10, whilst the options for the **Ruby / RSpec / Remote Control** Format are shown in Figure 9.11, whilst the settings for a user created format (**C++**) are shown in Figure 9.12.

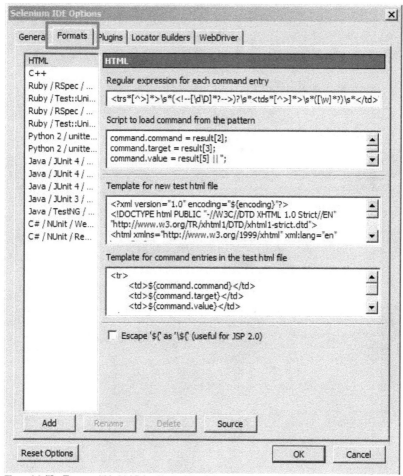

Figure 9.9. The **Formats** Tab (highlighted in Red Border).

As you can see from Figures 9.10 through 9.12, the different Formats have different options associated to them. One item that is common across all of the Formats is the **Source** Button (as shown in Figure 9.13).

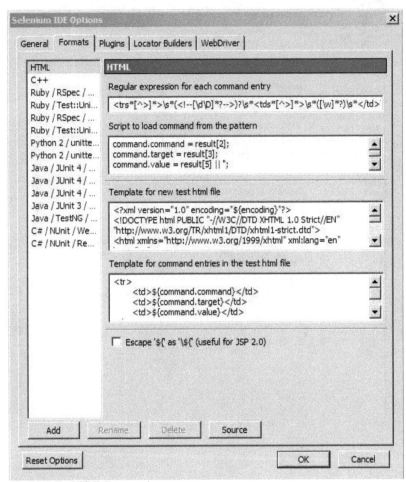

Figure 9.10. The **HTML** Format options.

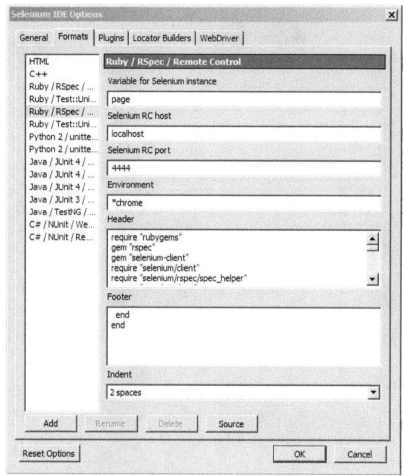

Figure 9.11. The **Ruby / RSpec / Remote Control** Format options.

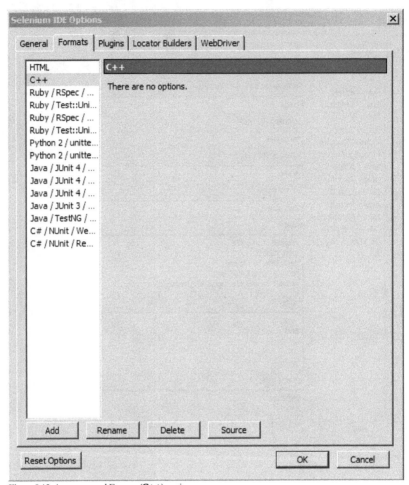

Figure 9.12. A user created Format (C++) options

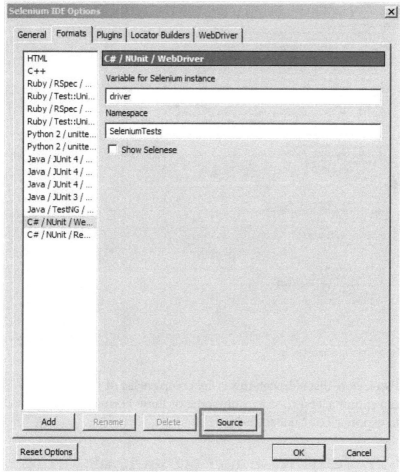

Figure 9.13. The **Source** Button (highlighted in Red Border).

Clicking the Source Button will load the **Source** Dialog (as shown in Figure 9.14). This will show the coding that is applied to ensure that the Selenium IDE code is exported into the correct Format.

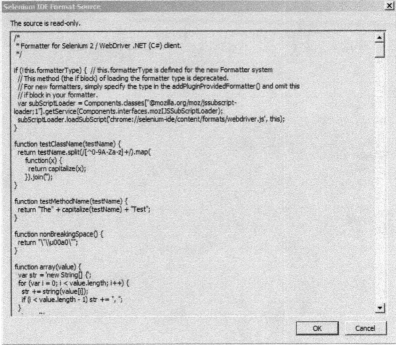

Figure 9.14. The **Source** Dialog.

Please note that although this is the complete list of Formats that you can export a Test Case to, only some of these Formats will allow you to export a Test Suite to them.

9.5 Adding a new Format to export to

As well as the standard Formats that are shipped with Selenium IDE, it is possible to create additional Formats. This is achieved by firstly clicking the **Add** Button (Figure 9.15)

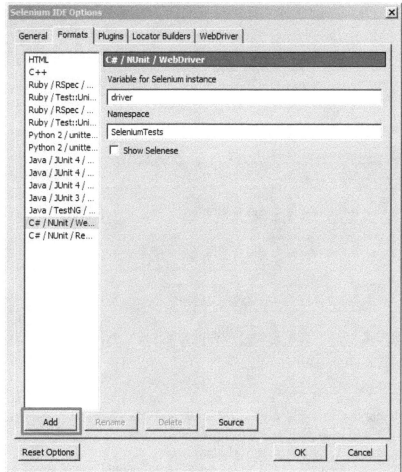

Figure 9.15. The **Add** Button (highlighted in Red Border).

Clicking the Add Button will load the **Format Source** Dialog (as shown in Figure 9.16). You can use the Format Source Dialog to enter the **Name Of The Format** (Figure 9.17) and also enter the formatting code (Figure 9.18).

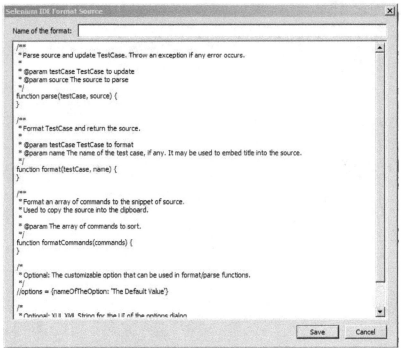

Figure 8916. The **Format Source** Dialog.

The Name Of The Format, needs to be unique, and should be descriptive of both the Format Language (e.g. Ruby, Python, Java, etc.) and also the versions of Selenium being exported to (e.g. Selenium RC or Selenium WebDriver).

A good example of a descriptive name would be **C++ For Selenium RC**.

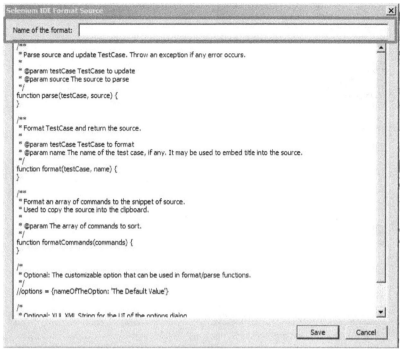

Figure 9.17. The **Name Of The Format** Textbox (in Red Border).

The Format Coding is very complicated to learn and it is recommended that initially, you copy the Format Coding for another Format and paste that into your new Format, and then manually make whatever changes you need to make.

Once you have entered a Name Of The Format and populated the Format Coding you can click on the **Save** Button (Figure 9.19) to Save the new Format.

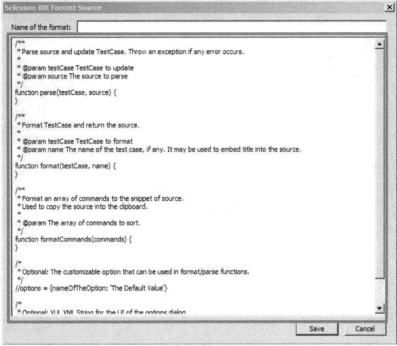

Figure 9.18. The **Format Source** Textbox (highlighted in Red Border).

Once saved, you will then need to close down and re-open the Options Dialog, for the new Format to be shown in the Formats List (as shown in Figure 9.20, which shows the newly create C++ For Selenium RC Format).

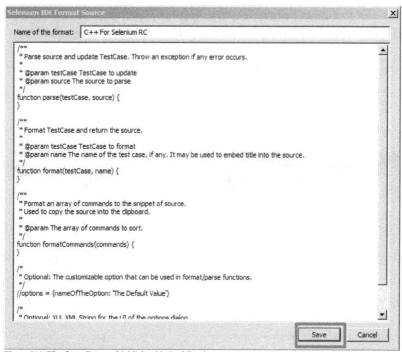

Figure 919. The **Save** Button (highlighted in Red Border).

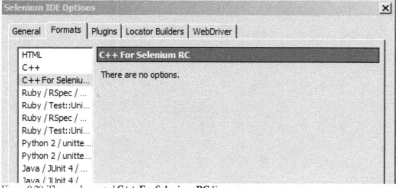

Figure 9.20. The newly created **C++ For Selenium RC** Format..

To see the new Format on the Export Test Case As Sub-Menu (Figure 9.21), you will need to close Selenium IDE and re-open it.

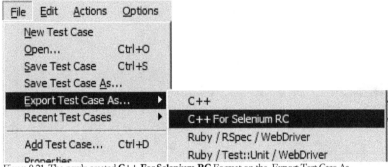

Figure 9.21. The newly created **C++ For Selenium RC** Format on the Export Test Case As..

Although you can add as many different Formats as you like, with the default set of Java, C#, Python, Ruby, and HTML it is unlikely you will need to add many new Formats, if any at all.

Chapter

10

Chapter 10: Approaches to implementing automation using Selenium IDE

We now have a discussion on how to implement automation using Selenium IDE.

In this chapter, we will discuss and identify the various ways in which you can implement automated testing using Selenium IDE. The Chapter covers:-

- Test Case Approach.
- Test Suite Approach.
- Export Approach.

10.1 Overview

There are multiple ways that you can use Selenium IDE to meet your automated testing needs, each has its' own benefits and drawbacks. We will concentrate on three main approaches in this chapter:

- Test Case Approach.
- Test Suite Approach.
- Export Approach.

In the following sections we will break-down each approach, giving more information about the approach, its' benefits and drawbacks. The approaches that are discussed are specific to Selenium IDE, so some may not be possible in other automation software.

10.2 Test Case Approach

The Test Case Approach is one where you record a collection of Test Cases. With each Test Case testing a specific bit of functionality. You would therefore record short bits of functionality as separate files.

When you come to playing-back the recordings you would get the Web Page to the point where the recording starts, load the Test

Case and then play-back the Test Case for it to test that functionality. Then load the next Test Case and do the same.

This approach will produce 1000s of small separate files, each with a separate small Test Case.

Some of the advantages of this approach are:

- It is quick to create 1000s of Test Cases and therefore get coverage of the Web Page functionality.
- It is a simple approach so can be done quickly.
- Changes to the Web Page functionality can be maintained by just deleting the Test Case and re-recording.

Some of the dis-advantages of this approach are:

- It is hard to maintain and manage so many files.
- Nothing is re-used, so work is duplicated.
- Play-back time takes much longer as you have to constantly load Test Cases.
- Play-back requires a lot of human interaction to load Test Cases.

10.3 Test Suite Approach

The Test Suite Approach is one where you record a collection of Test Cases, and create a series of Test Suites which are made-up of the recorded Test Cases. Again the individual Test Cases are testing a specific bit of functionality. You would therefore record short bits of functionality as Test Cases and join them into a Test Suite.

When you come to playing-back the recordings you would load the Test Suite and start from a known starting point e.g. logging into the Web Page, then let the Test Suite run through until completion.

This approach will result is 1000s of separate files for the Test Cases, and 100s of separate files for the Test Suite.

Some of the advantages of this approach are:

- It is quick to create 1000s of Test Cases and therefore get coverage of the Web Page functionality.
- It is a simple to add the Test Cases to Test Suites.
- Test Cases can be re-used.
- Changes to the Web Page functionality can be maintained by just editing the Test Case and re-recording.

Some of the dis-advantages of this approach are:

- Test Suites will become very large and difficult to maintain.
- Play-back time is long as the Test Suites will have many Test Cases and Commands to run.

10.4 Export Approach

The Export Approach is one where you record a Test Cases and then export the Test Case into a language such as Java or C#, etc. and use it in either Selenium RC or Selenium WebDriver. Therefore you build up a series of functions (in Java or C#, etc.) within Selenium RC or Selenium WebDriver which is your automated testing.

When you come to playing-back the recordings you would use Selenium RC or Selenium WebDriver to re-run the functionality.

Some of the advantages of this approach are:

- You could run the automated software against any Web Browser.
- The automated testing functions would be more robust.
- Play-back would be far quicker, than Selenium IDE.
- You could use Selenium Grid to run multiple tests at once.

Some of the dis-advantages of this approach are:

- This approach is much more complex than the other two approaches.
- A level of programming skills will be required.

10.5 Which Approach is right for you

Which approach is right for you? This is an almost impossible question to ask without knowing all your needs from automated testing, knowing the software you are testing, knowing the challenges you face, etc.

But generally, for which approach to use Selenium IDE for in automated Testing, the below rules will help. These rules are based upon the size and complexity of the Web software:

- For very small and very simple Web software the Test Case Approach (Section 10.2) would be best.
- For medium size and complex Web software the Test Suite Approach (Section 10.3) would be best.
- For larger and more complex Web software the Export Approach (Section 10.4) is most suited.

This is further broken down in Table 10.1, below.

Complexity / Size	Simple	Fairly Complex	Complex
Small	Test Case Approach	Test Case Approach **or** Test Suite Approach	Test Case Approach **or** Export Approach
Medium	Test Case Approach **or** Test Suite Approach	Test Suite Approach	Test Suite Approach **or** Export Approach
Large	Test Case Approach **or** Test Suite Approach	Test Suite Approach **or** Export Approach	Export Approach

Table 10.1. Table of best approach depending on Web software complexity and size.

Appendix

A

Appendix A: List of Selenium IDE Commands

Contained in this Appendix is the complete list of Selenium IDE Commands.

addLocationStrategy
addLocationStrategyAndWait
addScript
addScriptAndWait
addSelection
addSelectionAndWait
allowNativeXpath
allowNativeXpathAndWait
altKeyDown
altKeyDownAndWait
altKeyUp
altKeyUpAndWait
answerOnNextPrompt
assertAlert
assertAlertNotPresent
assertAlertPresent
assertAllButtons
assertAllFields
assertAllLinks
assertAllWindowIds
assertAllWindowNames
assertAllWindowTitles
assertAttribute
assertAttributeFromAllWindows
assertBodyText
assertChecked
assertConfirmation
assertConfirmationNotPresent
assertConfirmationPresent

assertCookie
assertCookieByName
assertCookieNotPresent
assertCookiePresent
assertCursorPosition
assertEditable
assertElementHeight
assertElementIndex
assertElementNotPresent
assertElementPositionLeft
assertElementPositionTop
assertElementPresent
assertElementWidth
assertEval
assertExpression
assertHtmlSource
assertLocation
assertMouseSpeed
assertNotAlert
assertNotAllButtons
assertNotAllFields
assertNotAllLinks
assertNotAllWindowIds
assertNotAllWindowNames
assertNotAllWindowTitles
assertNotAttribute
assertNotAttributeFromAllWindows
assertNotBodyText
assertNotChecked

assertNotConfirmation
assertNotCookie
assertNotCookieByName
assertNotCursorPosition
assertNotEditable
assertNotElementHeight
assertNotElementIndex
assertNotElementPositionLeft
assertNotElementPositionTop
assertNotElementWidth
assertNotEval
assertNotExpression
assertNotHtmlSource
assertNotLocation
assertNotMouseSpeed
assertNotOrdered
assertNotPrompt
assertNotSelectOptions
assertNotSelectedId
assertNotSelectedIds
assertNotSelectedIndex
assertNotSelectedIndexes
assertNotSelectedLabel
assertNotSelectedLabels
assertNotSelectedValue
assertNotSelectedValucs
assertNotSomethingSelected
assertNotSpeed
assertNotTable

assertNotText
assertNotTitle
assertNotValue
assertNotVisible
assertNotWhetherThisFrameMatchFrameExpression
assertNotWhetherThisWindowMatchWindowExpression
assertNotXpathCount
assertOrdered
assertPrompt
assertPromptNotPresent
assertPromptPresent
assertSelectOptions
assertSelectedId
assertSelectedIds
assertSelectedIndex
assertSelectedIndexes
assertSelectedLabel
assertSelectedLabels
assertSelectedValue
assertSelectedValues
assertSomethingSelected
assertSpeed
assertTable
assertText
assertTextNotPresent
assertTextPresent
assertTitle
assertValue
assertVisible

assertWhetherThisFrameMatchFrameExpression
assertWhetherThisWindowMatchWindowExpression
assertXpathCount
assignId
assignIdAndWait
break
captureEntirePageScreenshot
captureEntirePageScreenshotAndWait
check
checkAndWait
chooseCancelOnNextConfirmation
chooseOkOnNextConfirmation
chooseOkOnNextConfirmationAndWait
click
clickAndWait
clickAt
clickAtAndWait
close
contextMenu
contextMenuAndWait
contextMenuAt
contextMenuAtAndWait
controlKeyDown
controlKeyDownAndWait
controlKeyUp
controlKeyUpAndWait
createCookie
createCookieAndWait
deleteAllVisibleCookies

deleteAllVisibleCookiesAndWait
deleteCookie
deleteCookieAndWait
deselectPopUp
deselectPopUpAndWait
doubleClick
doubleClickAndWait
doubleClickAt
doubleClickAtAndWait
dragAndDrop
dragAndDropAndWait
dragAndDropToObject
dragAndDropToObjectAndWait
dragdrop
dragdropAndWait
echo
fireEvent
fireEventAndWait
focus
focusAndWait
goBack
goBackAndWait
highlight
highlightAndWait
ignoreAttributesWithoutValue
ignoreAttributesWithoutValueAndWait
keyDown
keyDownAndWait
keyPress

keyPressAndWait
keyUp
keyUpAndWait
metaKeyDown
metaKeyDownAndWait
metaKeyUp
metaKeyUpAndWait
mouseDown
mouseDownAndWait
mouseDownAt
mouseDownAtAndWait
mouseDownRight
mouseDownRightAndWait
mouseDownRightAt
mouseDownRightAtAndWait
mouseMove
mouseMoveAndWait
mouseMoveAt
mouseMoveAtAndWait
mouseOut
mouseOutAndWait
mouseOver
mouseOverAndWait
mouseUp
mouseUpAndWait
mouseUpAt
mouseUpAtAndWait
mouseUpRight
mouseUpRightAndWait

mouseUpRightAt
mouseUpRightAtAndWait
open
openWindow
openWindowAndWait
pause
refresh
refreshAndWait
removeAllSelections
removeAllSelectionsAndWait
removeScript
removeScriptAndWait
removeSelection
removeSelectionAndWait
rollup
rollupAndWait
runScript
runScriptAndWait
select
selectAndWait
selectFrame
selectPopUp
selectPopUpAndWait
selectWindow
sendKeys
setBrowserLogLevel
setBrowserLogLevelAndWait
setCursorPosition
setCursorPositionAndWait

setMouseSpeed
setMouseSpeedAndWait
setSpeed
setSpeedAndWait
setTimeout
shiftKeyDown
shiftKeyDownAndWait
shiftKeyUp
shiftKeyUpAndWait
store
storeAlert
storeAlertPresent
storeAllButtons
storeAllFields
storeAllLinks
storeAllWindowIds
storeAllWindowNames
storeAllWindowTitles
storeAttribute
storeAttributeFromAllWindows
storeBodyText
storeChecked
storeConfirmation
storeConfirmationPresent
storeCookie
storeCookieByName
storeCookiePresent
storeCursorPosition
storeEditable

storeElementHeight
storeElementIndex
storeElementPositionLeft
storeElementPositionTop
storeElementPresent
storeElementWidth
storeEval
storeExpression
storeHtmlSource
storeLocation
storeMouseSpeed
storeOrdered
storePrompt
storePromptPresent
storeSelectOptions
storeSelectedId
storeSelectedIds
storeSelectedIndex
storeSelectedIndexes
storeSelectedLabel
storeSelectedLabels
storeSelectedValue
storeSelectedValues
storeSomethingSelected
storeSpeed
storeTable
storeText
storeTextPresent
storeTitle

storeValue
storeVisible
storeWhetherThisFrameMatchFrameExpression
storeWhetherThisWindowMatchWindowExpression
storeXpathCount
submit
submitAndWait
type
typeAndWait
typeKeys
typeKeysAndWait
uncheck
uncheckAndWait
useXpathLibrary
useXpathLibraryAndWait
verifyAlert
verifyAlertNotPresent
verifyAlertPresent
verifyAllButtons
verifyAllFields
verifyAllLinks
verifyAllWindowIds
verifyAllWindowNames
verifyAllWindowTitles
verifyAttribute
verifyAttributeFromAllWindows
verifyBodyText
verifyChecked
verifyConfirmation

verifyConfirmationNotPresent
verifyConfirmationPresent
verifyCookie
verifyCookieByName
verifyCookieNotPresent
verifyCookiePresent
verifyCursorPosition
verifyEditable
verifyElementHeight
verifyElementIndex
verifyElementNotPresent
verifyElementPositionLeft
verifyElementPositionTop
verifyElementPresent
verifyElementWidth
verifyEval
verifyExpression
verifyHtmlSource
verifyLocation
verifyMouseSpeed
verifyNotAlert
verifyNotAllButtons
verifyNotAllFields
verifyNotAllLinks
verifyNotAllWindowIds
verifyNotAllWindowNames
verifyNotAllWindowTitles
verifyNotAttribute
verifyNotAttributeFromAllWindows

verifyNotBodyText
verifyNotChecked
verifyNotConfirmation
verifyNotCookie
verifyNotCookieByName
verifyNotCursorPosition
verifyNotEditable
verifyNotElementHeight
verifyNotElementIndex
verifyNotElementPositionLeft
verifyNotElementPositionTop
verifyNotElementWidth
verifyNotEval
verifyNotExpression
verifyNotHtmlSource
verifyNotLocation
verifyNotMouseSpeed
verifyNotOrdered
verifyNotPrompt
verifyNotSelectOptions
verifyNotSelectedId
verifyNotSelectedIds
verifyNotSelectedIndex
verifyNotSelectedIndexes
verifyNotSelectedLabel
verifyNotSelectedLabels
verifyNotSelectedValue
verifyNotSelectedValues
verifyNotSomethingSelected

verifyNotSpeed
verifyNotTable
verifyNotText
verifyNotTitle
verifyNotValue
verifyNotVisible
verifyNotWhetherThisFrameMatchFrameExpression
verifyNotWhetherThisWindowMatchWindowExpression
verifyNotXpathCount
verifyOrdered
verifyPrompt
verifyPromptNotPresent
verifyPromptPresent
verifySelectOptions
verifySelectedId
verifySelectedIds
verifySelectedIndex
verifySelectedLabel
verifySelectedLabels
verifySelectedValue
verifySelectedValues
verifySomethingSelected
verifySpeed
verifyTable
verifyText
verifyTextNotPresent
verifyTextPresent
verifyTitle
verifyValue

verifyVisible
verifyWhetherThisFrameMatchFrameExpression
verifyWhetherThisWindowMatchWindowExpression
verifyXpathCount
waitForAlert
waitForAlertNotPresent
waitForAlertPresent
waitForAllButtons
waitForAllFields
waitForAllLinks
waitForAllWindowIds
waitForAllWindowNames
waitForAllWindowTitles
waitForAttribute
waitForAttributeFromAllWindows
waitForBodyText
waitForChecked
waitForCondition
waitForConfirmation
waitForConfirmationNotPresent
waitForConfirmationPresent
waitForCookie
waitForCookieByName
waitForCookieNotPresent
waitForCookiePresent
waitForCursorPosition
waitForEditable
waitForElementHeight
waitForElementIndex

waitForElementNotPresent
waitForElementPositionLeft
waitForElementPositionTop
waitForElementPresent
waitForElementWidth
waitForEval
waitForExpression
waitForFrameToLoad
waitForHtmlSource
waitForLocation
waitForMouseSpeed
waitForNotAlert
waitForNotAllButtons
waitForNotAllFields
waitForNotAllLinks
waitForNotAllWindowIds
waitForNotAllWindowNames
waitForNotAllWindowTitles
waitForNotAttribute
waitForNotAttributeFromAllWindows
waitForNotBodyText
waitForNotChecked
waitForNotConfirmation
waitForNotCookie
waitForNotCookieByName
waitForNotCursorPosition
waitForNotEditable
waitForNotElementHeight
waitForNotElementIndex

waitForNotElementPositionLeft
waitForNotElementPositionTop
waitForNotElementWidth
waitForNotEval
waitForNotExpression
waitForNotHtmlSource
waitForNotLocation
waitForNotMouseSpeed
waitForNotOrdered
waitForNotPrompt
waitForNotSelectOptions
waitForNotSelectedId
waitForNotSelectedIds
waitForNotSelectedIndex
waitForNotSelectedIndexes
waitForNotSelectedLabel
waitForNotSelectedLabels
waitForNotSelectedValue
waitForNotSelectedValues
waitForNotSomethingSelected
waitForNotSpeed
waitForNotTable
waitForNotText
waitForNotTitle
waitForNotValue
waitForNotVisible
waitForNotWhetherThisFrameMatchFrameExpression
waitForNotWhetherThisWindowMatchWindowExpression
waitForNotXpathCount

waitForOrdered
waitForPageToLoad
waitForPopUp
waitForPrompt
waitForPromptNotPresent
waitForPromptPresent
waitForSelectOptions
waitForSelectedId
waitForSelectedIds
waitForSelectedIndex
waitForSelectedIndexes
waitForSelectedLabel
waitForSelectedLabels
waitForSelectedValue
waitForSelectedValues
waitForSomethingSelected
waitForSpeed
waitForTable
waitForText
waitForTextNotPresent
waitForTextPresent
waitForTitle
waitForValue
waitForVisible
waitForWhetherThisFrameMatchFrameExpression
waitForWhetherThisWindowMatchWindowExpression
waitForXpathCount
windowFocus
windowFocusAndWait

windowMaximize
windowMaximizeAndWait

Mark Chatham is an IT professional, who has been working in the IT industry for 15 years. His education background includes both BSc and MSc Degrees in Computer Science, as well MCP and ISEB professional Certifications.

During his professional IT career he has gained experience in the following technologies:

Development Langauges:
C, C++, C#, Java, Visual Basic.NET, SQL, XML.

Database Management Systems:
Microsoft SQL Server, Sybase SQL Anywhere, Microsoft Access, Ingres SQL.

Automation Testing Tools:
Selenium IDE, RC, Web Driver, QTP, Telerik Web UI, InCisif .NET, JMeter, OWASP.

The author can be contacted via email on:
mchatham@hotmail.co.uk

(Please ensure any comments or questions relating to this book, have the Subject text of "**Selenium By Example – Volume I: Selenium IDE**").

Related Titles

The following titles are from the **Selenium By Example** series of books, and are from the same author:

- **Selenium By Example – Volume II: Selenium Remote Control.**
  This title gives a step-by-step overview of Selenium Remote Control.

- **Selenium By Example – Volume III: Selenium WebDriver.**
  This title gives a step-by-step overview of Selenium WebDriver.

- **Selenium By Example – Volume IV: Selenium Grid.**
  This title gives a step-by-step overview of Selenium Grid.

All title follow the same example based method to teach the reader the necessary information in a step-by-step way. This is to ensure that the reader is able to quickly and efficiently learn the new information presented. The following titles